MAINE
STATE PARKS ^{BUCKET} LIST

Max Kukis Galgan

ISBN: 9798396918924

ABOUT MAINE

Maine, located in the northeastern region of the United States, is the easternmost state in the New England area. It shares borders with New Hampshire to the west, the Gulf of Maine to the southeast, and the Canadian provinces of New Brunswick and Quebec to the northeast and northwest respectively. Among the New England states, Maine boasts the largest total area but is the 12th smallest in terms of land area. It ranks as the 9th least populous and the 13th least densely populated state, with a predominantly rural landscape. Additionally, Maine is the northeasternmost state within the contiguous United States, the northernmost state east of the Great Lakes, the only state with a one-syllable name, and the sole state that shares a border with just one other U.S. state. Roughly half of Maine's land lies on each side of the 45th parallel north in latitude. The most populous city in Maine is Portland, and its capital is Augusta.

Maine has gained recognition for its rugged and rocky coastlines along the Atlantic Ocean and bays, as well as its smoothly shaped mountains, densely forested interior, scenic waterways, and notable culinary offerings such as wild lowbush blueberries and seafood delicacies, particularly lobster and clams. The coastal and Down East regions of Maine have become significant hubs for the creative economy, with Portland and its surrounding areas experiencing gentrification.

The land of Maine has been inhabited by indigenous populations for thousands of years, ever since the glaciers receded during the last ice age. When Europeans arrived, the area was governed by several Algonquian-speaking nations, which are now collectively known as the Wabanaki Confederacy. The French established the first European settlement in 1604 on Saint Croix Island, led by Pierre Dugua, Sieur de Mons. The first English settlement, called the Popham Colony, was established in 1607 by the Plymouth Company. In the 1620s, several English settlements were established along the Maine coast, but many of them failed due to the harsh climate and conflicts with the local indigenous people. By the 18th century, only a few European settlements in Maine had survived. During the American Revolution, both Loyalist and Patriot forces fought for control of Maine's territory. In the War of 1812, the eastern region of Maine, which was largely undefended, was occupied by British forces with the intention of annexing it to Canada through the Colony of New Ireland. However, the British offensives on the northern border, mid-Atlantic, and southern regions failed, and as a result of a peace treaty, the occupied territory was returned to the United States, restoring the pre-war boundaries. Maine was initially part of the Commonwealth of Massachusetts until 1820 when it voted to secede from Massachusetts and become an independent state. On March 15, 1820, under the Missouri Compromise, Maine was admitted to the Union as the 23rd state.

Maine falls within the temperate broadleaf and mixed forests biome. The region along the southern and central Atlantic coast is characterized by mixed oak trees that belong to the Northeastern coastal forests. The rest of the state, including the North Woods, is covered by the New England–Acadian forests. With a coastline stretching nearly 230 miles (400 km) and a tidal coastline extending 3,500 miles (5,600 km), Maine is abundant in coastal beauty. The easternmost point of land in the contiguous 48 states can be found at West Quoddy Head in Lubec. Along the renowned rocky coastline of Maine, one can find lighthouses, beaches, fishing villages, and a multitude of offshore islands, including the Isles of Shoals that lie partially in New Hampshire. The area is characterized by rugged rocks, cliffs, numerous bays, and inlets. Inland, there are lakes, rivers, forests, and mountains.

Geologists characterize the landscape of Maine as a "drowned coast," resulting from the rising sea levels that have encroached upon former land formations. This process has transformed valleys into bays and mountain tops into islands. The melting of heavy glacier ice caused a rise in land elevation, leading to a slight rebound effect on the underlying rock. However, this rise was insufficient to fully counteract the impact of the rising sea levels and their invasion of previously existing land features.

Maine experiences a humid continental climate. The state is characterized by warm and occasionally humid summers, as well as long, cold, and heavily snowy winters. Winters, particularly in the northern and western parts of Maine, are especially harsh. However, coastal areas benefit from some moderation due to the influence of the Atlantic Ocean, resulting in relatively milder winters and cooler summers compared to inland regions. In July, daytime temperatures typically range from 75 to 85 °F (24 to 29 °C) throughout the state, while nighttime temperatures hover around the high 50s °F (approximately 15 °C). In January, temperatures vary from highs near 30 °F (-1 °C) along the southern coast to overnight lows that average below 0 °F (-18 °C) in the far north. The highest recorded temperature in Maine is 105 °F (41 °C), which was set in July 1911 in North Bridgton. Precipitation in Maine is generally evenly distributed throughout the year, although there is a slight summer peak in the northern and northwestern parts of the state, as well as a slight late-fall or early-winter peak along the coast due to the influence of "nor'easters" or intense rain and snowstorms during the colder months. Coastal Maine experiences its driest period during late spring and summer, which is unusual compared to other parts of the Eastern United States. Maine has fewer thunderstorm days than any other state east of the Rockies, with most areas averaging fewer than twenty days of thunderstorms per year. Tornadoes are infrequent in Maine, with an average of two per year, although this number appears to be increasing. The majority of severe thunderstorms and tornadoes occur in the southwestern interior of the state, where summer temperatures tend to be the warmest and the atmosphere is more unstable compared to the northern and coastal regions. Maine rarely experiences direct landfall from tropical cyclones, as they typically veer out to sea or weaken significantly by the time they reach the cooler waters of Maine.

Tourism and outdoor activities are significant and growing contributors to Maine's economy. The state is a highly sought-after destination for various recreational pursuits, including sport hunting (especially for deer, moose, and bear), sport fishing, snowmobiling, skiing, boating, camping, and hiking. These activities attract visitors from near and far.

During the summer season, Maine offers an exceptional experience that is hard to beat. With a diverse range of attractions, from picturesque beaches to breathtaking mountains, there is an abundance of opportunities for exploration and enjoyment. The sheer variety of options might leave you unsure of where to begin your adventure. However, rest assured that you have arrived at the perfect destination to embark on your summer escapades. Whether your preferred activities involve cycling or kayaking, hiking or biking, Maine offers an abundance of outdoor spaces that are ideal for making the most of the extended summer daylight hours.

PARK NAME	COUNTY	EST.	VISITED
Allagash Wilderness Waterway	Aroostook	1966	
Androscoggin Riverlands	Franklin, Oxford	-	
Aroostook State Park	Aroostook	1939	
Baxter State Park	Piscataquis	1930	
Birch Point State Park	Knox	1999	
Bradbury Mountain State Park	Cumberland	1939	
Camden Hills State Park	Knox	1947	
Cobscook Bay State Park	Washington	1964	
Crescent Beach State Park	Cumberland	1966	
Damariscotta Lake State Park	Lincoln	1970	
Ferry Beach State Park	York	-	
Fort Point State Park	Waldo	1974	
Grafton Notch State Park	Oxford	1963	
Holbrook Island Sanctuary State Park	Hancock	1971	
Lake St. George State Park	Waldo	-	
Lamoine State Park	Hancock	1950s	
Lily Bay State Park	Piscataquis	1959	
Mackworth Island	Cumberland	1946	
Moose Point State Park	Waldo	1963	
Mount Blue State Park	Franklin	1955	
Mount Kineo State Park	Piscataquis	-	
Owls Head Light State Park	Knox	1978	
Peaks-Kenny State Park	Piscataquis	1969	
Penobscot Narrows Observatory	Hancock	1931	
Penobscot River Corridor	Penobscot	-	
Popham Beach State Park	Sagadahoc	-	
Quoddy Head State Park	Washington	1962	
Range Ponds State Park	Androscoggin	1965	

PARK NAME	COUNTY	EST.	VISITED
Rangeley Lake State Park	Franklin	1960	
Reid State Park	Sagadahoc	1950	
Roque Bluffs State Park	Washington	1969	
Scarborough Beach State Park	Cumberland	-	
Sebago Lake State Park	Cumberland	1938	
Shackford Head State Park	Washington	1989	
Swan Lake State Park	Waldo	-	
Swans Falls Campground	Oxford	-	
Two Lights State Park	Cumberland	1961	
Vaughan Woods Memorial State Park	York	1949	
Warren Island State Park	Waldo	1959	
Wolfe's Neck Woods State Park	Cumberland	1972	
HISTORIC SITES			
Bible Point State Historic Site	Penobscot	1971	
Colburn House State Historic Site	Kennebec	1971	
Colonial Pemaquid State Historic Site (Ft. William Henry)	Lincoln	1969	
Eagle Island State Historic Site	Cumberland	1967	
Fort Baldwin State Historic Site	Sagadahoc	1979	
Fort Edgecomb State Historic Site	Lincoln	1969	
Fort Halifax State Historic Site	Kennebec	1968	
Fort Kent State Historic Site	Aroostook	1969	
Fort Knox State Historic Site	Waldo	1969	
Fort McClary State Historic Site	York	1969	
Fort O'Brien State Historic Site	Washington	1923	
Fort Popham State Historic Site	Sagadahoc	1969	
Katahdin Iron Works	Piscataquis	1969	
Storer Garrison State Historic Site	York	-	
Whaleback Shell Midden	Lincoln	1969	

COUNTY	PARK NAME	EST.	VISITED
Androscoggin	Range Ponds State Park	1965	
Aroostook	Allagash Wilderness Waterway	1966	
Aroostook	Aroostook State Park	1939	
Cumberland	Bradbury Mountain State Park	1939	
Cumberland	Crescent Beach State Park	1966	
Cumberland	Mackworth Island	1946	
Cumberland	Scarborough Beach State Park	-	
Cumberland	Sebago Lake State Park	1938	
Cumberland	Two Lights State Park	1961	
Cumberland	Wolfe's Neck Woods State Park	1972	
Franklin	Mount Blue State Park	1955	
Franklin	Rangeley Lake State Park	1960	
Franklin, Oxford	Androscoggin Riverlands	-	
Hancock	Holbrook Island Sanctuary State Park	1971	
Hancock	Lamoine State Park	1950s	
Hancock	Penobscot Narrows Observatory	1931	
Knox	Birch Point State Park	1999	
Knox	Camden Hills State Park	1947	
Knox	Owls Head Light State Park	1978	
Lincoln	Damariscotta Lake State Park	1970	
Oxford	Grafton Notch State Park	1963	
Oxford	Swans Falls Campground	-	
Penobscot	Penobscot River Corridor	-	
Piscataquis	Baxter State Park	1930	
Piscataquis	Lily Bay State Park	1959	
Piscataquis	Mount Kineo State Park	-	
Piscataquis	Peaks-Kenny State Park	1969	
Sagadahoc	Popham Beach State Park	-	

COUNTY	PARK NAME	EST.	VISITED
Sagadahoc	Reid State Park	1950	
Waldo	Fort Point State Park	1974	
Waldo	Lake St. George State Park	-	
Waldo	Moose Point State Park	1963	
Waldo	Swan Lake State Park	-	
Waldo	Warren Island State Park	1959	
Washington	Cobscook Bay State Park	1964	
Washington	Quoddy Head State Park	1962	
Washington	Roque Bluffs State Park	1969	
Washington	Shackford Head State Park	1989	
York	Ferry Beach State Park	-	
York	Vaughan Woods Memorial State Park	1949	
HISTORIC SITES			
Aroostook	Fort Kent State Historic Site	1969	
Cumberland	Eagle Island State Historic Site	1967	
Kennebec	Colburn House State Historic Site	1971	
Kennebec	Fort Halifax State Historic Site	1968	
Lincoln	Colonial Pemaquid State Historic Site (Ft. William Henry)	1969	
Lincoln	Fort Edgecomb State Historic Site	1969	
Lincoln	Whaleback Shell Midden	1969	
Penobscot	Bible Point State Historic Site	1971	
Piscataquis	Katahdin Iron Works	1969	
Sagadahoc	Fort Baldwin State Historic Site	1979	
Sagadahoc	Fort Popham State Historic Site	1969	
Waldo	Fort Knox State Historic Site	1969	
Washington	Fort O'Brien State Historic Site	1923	
York	Fort McClary State Historic Site	1969	
York	Storer Garrison State Historic Site	-	

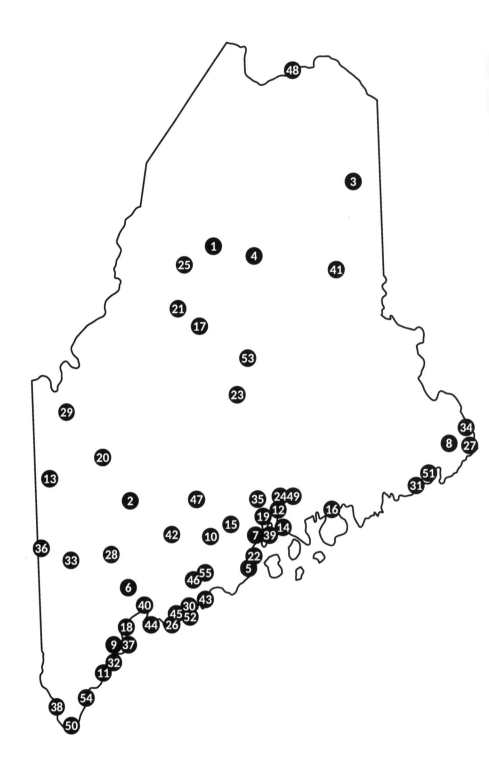

1 Allagash Wilderness Waterway

2 Androscoggin Riverlands

3 Aroostook State Park

4 Baxter State Park

5 Birch Point State Park

6 Bradbury Mountain State Park

7 Camden Hills State Park State Park

8 Cobscook Bay State Park

9 Crescent Beach State Park

10 Damariscotta Lake State Park

11 Ferry Beach State Park

12 Fort Point State Park

13 Grafton Notch State Park

14 Holbrook Island Sanctuary State Park

15 Lake St. George State Park

16 Lamoine State Park

17 Lily Bay State Park

18 Mackworth Island

19 Moose Point State Park

20 Mount Blue State Park

21 Mount Kineo State Park

22 Owls Head Light State Park

23 Peaks-Kenny State Park

24 Penobscot Narrows Observatory

25 Penobscot River Corridor

26 Popham Beach State Park

27 Quoddy Head State Park

28 Range Ponds State Park

29 Rangeley Lake State Park

30 Reid State Park

31 Roque Bluffs State Park

32 Scarborough Beach State Park

33 Sebago Lake State Park

34 Shackford Head State Park

35 Swan Lake State Park

36 Swans Falls Campground

37 Two Lights State Park

38 Vaughan Woods Memorial State Park

39 Warren Island State Park

40 Wolfe's Neck Woods State Park

41 Bible Point State Historic Site

42 Colburn House State Historic Site

43 Colonial Pemaquid State HS (Ft. William Henry)

44 Eagle Island State Historic Site

45 Fort Baldwin State Historic Site

46 Fort Edgecomb State Historic Site

47 Fort Halifax State Historic Site

48 Fort Kent State Historic Site

49 Fort Knox State Historic Site

50 Fort McClary State Historic Site

51 Fort O'Brien State Historic Site

52 Fort Popham State Historic Site

53 Katahdin Iron Works

54 Storer Garrison State Historic Site

55 Whaleback Shell Midden

INVENTORY

- BEAR SPRAY
- BINOCULARS
- CAMERA + ACCESSORIES
- CELL PHONE + CHARGER
- FIRST AID KIT
- FLASHLIGHT/ HEADLAMP
- FLEECE/ WATERPROOF JACKET
- GUIDE BOOK (THIS BOOK)
- HAND LOTION
- HAND SANITIZER
- HIKING SHOES
- INSECT REPELLENT
- LIP BALM
- MEDICATIONS AND PAINKILLERS
- SUNGLASSES
- SNACKS
- SPARE SOCKS
- SUN HAT
- SUNSCREEN
- TOILET PAPER
- TRASH BAGS
- WATER
- WATER SHOES/ SANDALS

ALLAGASH WILDERNESS WATERWAY

COUNTY: AROOSTOOK   ESTABLISHED: 1966   AREA (AC/HA): - / -

DATE VISITED: LODGING: WHO I WENT WITH:

WEATHER: ☀️☐ ☁️☐ 🌧️☐ ❄️☐ ⛈️☐ 🌊☐   SPRING ☐ SUMMER ☐ FALL ☐ WINTER ☐

FEE(S):   RATING: ☆ ☆ ☆ ☆ ☆   WILL I RETURN?   YES / NO

The Allagash Wilderness Waterway, is a renowned canoe route spanning 92 miles in northern Maine, was created by the Maine State Legislature in 1966 and recognized by the U.S. Department of the Interior in 1970 as the inaugural state-managed part of the National Wild and Scenic River System. In the past, the Allagash River, along with the connecting lakes and ponds, served as a remote and vital transportation route within the vast forests of northwestern Maine. It was heavily utilized by loggers, who would cut and float numerous logs down its waters for trade. However, nowadays, the Allagash River holds a different purpose: it attracts canoeists and kayakers who seek solitude and thrilling experiences in the furthest corners of the North Maine Woods. The region that once served as a prosperous source of wealth for numerous lumber industries has a history that stretches back even further. Archaeologists believe that Native American tribes were the first to settle in the area, with evidence suggesting their presence as early as ten centuries prior to the arrival of the lumbermen. After the last Ice Age, the landscape in northern Maine transitioned from a tundra-like environment to dense forests approximately 10,000 years ago. While a few Paleoindian families may have passed through the Allagash region during that time, archaeological findings indicate a larger population during the Archaic period, spanning from 10,000 to 4,000 years ago. The people of this era were predominantly nomadic, relying on fishing nets and stone or wooden tools. Stone axes and gouges used for woodworking are among the most abundant artifacts discovered from this period. Around 4,000 to 3,500 years ago, there was a decline in the prevalence of these tools, suggesting a shift from dugout canoes to birch bark canoes. This shift is further supported by the concentration of archaeological sites in drainage areas where heavier dugout canoes would have been less practical. The period known as the Ceramic Period, spanning from 3,000 to 500 years ago, derives its name from the significant development of pottery usage. While pottery from this time was not highly durable, it introduced the convenience of cooking directly over a fire, eliminating the labor-intensive practice of heating stones and placing them in bark or wooden containers. Although the Allagash region is not favorable for the preservation of ceramic artifacts over long periods, archaeologists have discovered pottery in the area that dates back at least 2,000 years. Dr. Art Spiess from the Maine Historic Preservation Commission explains that during most of prehistory, the Native American population in Maine sustained themselves through hunting, fishing, and gathering in small, band-organized societies without complex political structures. Native Americans in Maine historically had a relatively mobile lifestyle, living in smaller groups. The archaeological evidence suggests that traditional Native American communities began to move away from the Allagash region as early as the 1800s. The Allagash Wilderness Waterway is considered a quintessential destination for paddlers in the eastern United States. Explorers can embark on the entire route, spending over a week on the water, or opt for shorter, multi-day trips. Regardless of the journey's duration, boaters encounter vast and picturesque lakes, which can be serene or challenging with occasional strong winds, as well as river sections that flow gently or boast Class II whitewater rapids. In addition to the magnificent boating opportunities, the Allagash region provides excellent fishing grounds in Maine. Whether casting their lines from a boat or the shoreline, anglers can catch wild native brook trout, lake trout, and lake whitefish. During the winter, the Allagash becomes a prime location for ice fishing, attracting anglers who reach the fishing spots via snowmobiles. While the Waterway is surrounded by actively managed commercial forests, visitors will access the river using logging roads. However, the purpose of the Waterway is to create a sense of seclusion from the outside world for paddlers. Signs of modern civilization are scarce, and campgrounds along the water, although abundant, offer limited amenities. Expect basic accommodations such as tent spaces, tarp poles, outhouses, and a couple of picnic tables. This is a true backcountry camping experience where encounters with moose are more common than spotting someone with a working cellphone. Embarking on a northbound adventure along the Allagash River is not only a physical journey but also a voyage through history. Remnants of old logging and lumber equipment can be found scattered among the trees, including a tramway that was once used to transport logs through the forest. Additionally, two locomotives from the now-defunct Eagle Lake & West Branch Railroad, which transported hundreds of thousands of cords of wood, now rest where they were left, serving as reminders of the past. Completing the Allagash trip is a lifelong dream for many paddlers, but it can also be an intimidating one. Thorough planning is essential since travelers must bring everything they need for the journey. There are no convenience stores along the banks of the Allagash to restock supplies. Due to its challenging nature and remote environment, the Allagash is ideally suited for experienced paddlers who undertake the journey on their own. However, newcomers to the river can still enjoy it by participating in guided trips. On these guided journeys, the guides handle the planning and logistics while leading the way for the group, allowing participants to fully immerse themselves in the experience.

NOTES:

PASSPORT STAMPS

ANDROSCOGGIN RIVERLANDS

COUNTY: FRANKLIN, OXFORD	ESTABLISHED: -	AREA (AC/HA): 2,675 / 1,082
DATE VISITED:	LODGING:	WHO I WENT WITH:
WEATHER: ☀☐ ☁☐ 🌫☐ ❄☐ 🌧☐ ⛈☐		SPRING ☐ SUMMER ☐ FALL ☐ WINTER ☐
FEE(S):	RATING: ☆ ☆ ☆ ☆ ☆	WILL I RETURN? YES / NO

Located close to the urban area of Lewiston/Auburn, Androscoggin Riverlands State Park spans across 2,675 acres and boasts 12 miles of river frontage. It is the fifth largest park in the State and conveniently accessible to over half of Maine's population within an hour's drive. With its vast network of trails and untouched natural areas, the park provides ample opportunities for recreational activities and serves as a habitat for various wildlife species. Furthermore, it is connected to the larger Androscoggin Greenway and the Androscoggin River Water Trail, enhancing its significance and ecological value. Boating enthusiasts will also find delight in the park, as the river is a prominent feature, providing convenient access points and picturesque picnic areas. The park is open throughout the year, starting from 9:00 a.m. until sunset every day, unless there are specific instructions at the entrance. Currently, there is no fee required to enter this park. From the end of the snowmobile season until May 15, the park is gated and can only be accessed on foot. During winter, skiers and snowmobilers make use of the trails, while in the warmer seasons, people engage in a variety of activities such as hiking, boating, and riding ATVs (ATV use is permitted only between May 15 and December 15, unless stated otherwise). It is worth noting that hunting is a popular activity in these lands, so it is advisable to wear highly visible clothing during the autumn season. Turner Lands (2,345 acres): This section of the park, which is larger of the two, stretches across 6 miles along the western shore of the Androscoggin River in Turner. It features gently rolling terrain and offers a variety of recreational activities for visitors on foot, bicycle, ATV, or horseback. There are 12 miles of multi-use trails available, as well as an additional 10 miles of foot trails (6.6 miles of which are shared with single-track biking). These trails provide excellent opportunities for wildlife observation and spotting. Leeds Lands (330 acres): Situated along the eastern shore of the Androscoggin River, this section of the park consists of relatively flat and forested lands. Access to this area is primarily by boat, with canoes and kayaks being the preferred options due to shallow water. The Androscoggin, which is the third largest river in Maine, originates in the mountains of New Hampshire and flows for 164 miles, descending 1,500 vertical feet until it reaches Merrymeeting Bay. For over 9,000 years, Native Americans used to camp and fish along its shores, giving the river its name, which translates to "plenty of fish" or "fish coming in spring." The river's steep gradient, averaging 8 feet per mile, posed challenges for boat travel but also provided the necessary power for textile and paper mills. In 1925, the Gulf Island Dam was constructed in Auburn to generate hydropower, resulting in the creation of a 14-mile impoundment that led to the abandonment of settlements along the river. Industries located along the riverfront caused significant pollution, and by the 1960s, the Androscoggin was among the ten most polluted rivers in the United States. Pollutants accumulated behind the dams, causing a decline in water quality. However, the implementation of the Clean Water Act in 1972, along with subsequent reductions in industrial and municipal waste discharges, played a crucial role in significantly improving the water quality of the river. The preservation of the riverfront park as a natural area for public recreation and conservation was made possible through the dedicated efforts and commitment of community residents and organizations. A wide-ranging coalition, consisting of local municipalities, the Androscoggin Land Trust, the Androscoggin River Watershed Council, the Androscoggin River Alliance, the Androscoggin Valley Council of Governments, and the Maine Bureau of Parks and Lands, has come together to plan for the future of the river and the Androscoggin Greenway. Key players in the coalition, such as the Androscoggin Land Trust, The Nature Conservancy, and the Trust for Public Land, played crucial roles in negotiating land acquisitions. Additionally, the State's Land for Maine's Future Program and the National Park Service's Land and Water Conservation Fund provided essential support for land purchases. This collaborative effort demonstrates the shared commitment to preserving this valuable natural area for the benefit of the community and future generations. The Multi-Use Trail, spanning 9.5 miles in one direction, serves as the main pathway through the Turner parcel of the park. It is highly popular among various recreational users, including ATV riders, snowmobilers, bicyclists, horseback riders, and hikers. For off-loading their ATVs, it is necessary for users to utilize the north entrance parking area. The Homestead Trail offers a 4.5-mile loop with an optional shorter route of 2.6 miles. Allowing approximately 2.5 hours for the full loop, this trail provides a scenic riverside hiking experience. It begins at the northern parking lot and leads to the Picnic Meadow, covering a distance of 1.1 miles. From there, you can opt to take the "Harrington Trail," which is 0.5 miles long, before connecting back to the Multi-Use Trail for a 1.0-mile stretch leading back to the parking area. If you wish to extend your hike, continue south on the trail beyond the Picnic Meadow. This will take you to the junction with the Multi-Use Trail, which leads back to the main entrance. This additional section spans 1.8 miles and provides an opportunity to explore further along the trail. To access the Ridge Trail, follow the extended Homestead Trail until you reach the Multi-Use Trail, covering a distance of 2.0 miles. From there, turn left and cross a bridge, then take a right turn and continue uphill until you reach a ledge outcrop that offers a scenic view of the river, spanning approximately 1 mile. Next, take a left turn and descend steeply towards the river on the Ledges Trail, which is 0.4 miles long. After reaching the bottom, take a left turn onto the Multi-Use Trail and continue for 2.25 miles until you reach the Picnic Meadow. From there, you can return to the parking area by following the Homestead Trail, covering a distance of 1.1 miles. The Deer Path Trail offers an additional loop beyond the Ledges Trail and adds approximately 8.0 miles to your hike. This trail includes the Bradford Loop Trail, which is 0.5 miles long and connects with the Deer Path Trail. After approximately 1.5 miles on the Deer Path Trail, bear right at a fork and continue for 0.5 miles until you reach the Multi-Use Trail. Finally, return to the starting point by following the Homestead Trail for 2.0 miles. The Bradford Loop Trail is a challenging 12.2-mile loop that is suitable for advanced ATV riders and snowmobilers. It can be accessed from the north end of the park by following the Multi-Use Trail. The Bradford Hill Trail offers hiking opportunities and has variable trip lengths. To begin a 9.6-mile loop hike, enter the park through the Conant Road entrance. Follow the Multi-Use Trail for approximately 3.8 miles, then take a left turn onto the Bradford Hill Trail. Afterward, make a right turn onto the Bradford Loop Technical Trail and continue until you reach the Multi-Use Trail again, which will lead you back to the parking area. The Pine Loop Trail, starting from the Conant Road parking lot, is a round trip covering approximately 5.7 miles. This trail runs alongside the river, providing scenic views. Begin by hiking along the Multi-Use Primitive Trail for 1.6 miles (please refer to the map as this section of the trail may be rough), and then veer right to connect with the Pine Loop Trail. When engaging in boating or hiking activities, it is important to come prepared. Ensure you have extra clothing, including appropriate footwear, as well as a map and compass for navigation. It is also crucial to bring an ample supply of water and food. Additionally, make sure to inform someone of your planned destination and expected return time for safety purposes. The park strictly prohibits the use of intoxicating beverages. Fires are only allowed in designated day-use areas that have fire rings, and it is essential to avoid cutting any live vegetation. Visitors need to ensure that all trash is carried out of the park. To protect sensitive ecosystems, it is important to stay on designated trails while exploring the park. When observing wildlife, maintain a safe distance that does not disturb their natural behavior. Refrain from following or feeding the animals. Discharging weapons is strictly prohibited within 300 feet of any picnic area, parking area, posted trail, or other developed areas. Hiking trails do not allow loaded firearms. Pets must be kept on a leash that is shorter than 4 feet at all times, and they should not be left unattended. ATVs are required to use the north entrance parking area for off-loading purposes.

NOTES:

PASSPORT STAMPS

AROOSTOOK STATE PARK

COUNTY: AROOSTOOK	ESTABLISHED: 1939		AREA (AC/HA): 910 / 368
DATE VISITED:	LODGING:	WHO I WENT WITH:	
WEATHER: ☀️☐ ☁️☐ 🌧️☐ ❄️☐ ⛅☐ 🌊☐		SPRING ☐ SUMMER ☐ FALL ☐ WINTER ☐	
FEE(S):	RATING: ☆ ☆ ☆ ☆ ☆	WILL I RETURN? YES / NO	

Aroostook State Park, the first state park in Maine, is situated on Echo Lake in the heart of Maine's potato region. Popular activities in the park include hiking on Quaggy Jo Mountain, fishing for trout in Echo Lake, and camping. The park's natural areas exemplify the typical landscape of northern Maine. The forest primarily consists of a mixture of spruce, fir, beech, and maple trees, while cedar stands can be found in low, marshy areas. Various species of birds and mammals inhabit the park, with squirrels and chipmunks being the most commonly observed. However, foxes, deer, moose, and bears also make the park their home. Additionally, a diverse range of birds, including hawks, owls, and woodpeckers, can be found in the area. Echo Lake, which is fed by springs, is home to large brook trout, particularly during the spring season. This is a well-liked recreational area throughout all four seasons. The park offers a variety of outdoor activities, including hiking, skiing, fishing, swimming, and camping. The best time for fishing is from spring ice-out until mid-June. Visitors should be cautious of bears with cubs and be prepared for black flies. Bird enthusiasts can enjoy the park's birdwatching opportunities year-round. During the summer, hikers can appreciate the picturesque views, diverse trails, and camping options. Echo Lake is a popular spot for swimming, canoeing, and kayaking, and the park provides a limited number of watercraft available for rent. In autumn, the park showcases spectacular fall foliage, typically best viewed from mid-September to the first week of October. It is advisable to wear blaze orange during hunting season. During winter, snowshoers and cross-country skiers can find beauty and solitude on the park's trails, which include 15 miles of cross-country skiing trails and 6.5 miles of snowshoeing trails. Snowmobilers can also cross the park using ITS-83. Quaggy Jo Mountain, the most notable feature of Aroostook State Park, stands prominently above the surrounding farmlands. Shaped over time by geological processes such as folding of the Earth's crust and glaciations, Quaggy Jo Mountain offers a unique opportunity to study our planet's geological history. The underlying limestone formations indicate the presence of an ancient sea, while the outer layer of volcanic rock suggests a later lava flow with an unknown origin. The name "Quaggy Jo" is a shortened version of its original Indian name, "Qua Qua Jo," which translates to "twin peaked." Aroostook County, known as the "Crown of Maine," is famous for its potato cultivation. For generations, it has also been a beloved destination during winter. In the early fall of 1938, the Presque Isle Merchants Association presented a deed for the initial 100 acres of land at Quoggy Joe Mountain (now Quaggy Jo Mountain) to the state, marking the establishment of Maine's first state park. By the middle of fall, funds were raised, plans were made, an engineer was hired, and the Works Progress Administration (WPA) was enlisted to develop a ski trail and winter sports programs. In November, Elbridge Sprague, a long-time resident, broke ground for a new ski trail, and a crew of 35 WPA workers began clearing the trail on the mountain's east side. By the end of December, the half-mile trail was completed and ready for use, and by February 1939, downhill and slalom skiers were registering for races. The park offers 30 campsites nestled in wooded areas, each equipped with a picnic table and fire pit. Campers have access to amenities such as hot showers, flush toilets, and a kitchen shelter with electricity and water. Additionally, there are two group camping sites available. For boating enthusiasts, the park provides both a trailerable boat launch and a hand-carry boat launch. More information can be found at www.maine.gov/dacf/boatlaunches. During the summer season, canoe and kayak rentals are available. Picnic areas are located along the shores of Echo Lake. Children can have fun on the swing set provided in the park. There is a plentiful presence of moose, bears, and other large animals in the area. It is important to observe them from a safe distance and avoid startling or disturbing the wildlife. When driving, it is recommended to maintain a slow speed, especially during periods of low light. When camping, it is crucial to securely store food to prevent attracting animals. Tents should be kept free of food and any lingering food odors to avoid attracting wildlife. When visiting Aroostook State Park, it is important to follow the visitor rules to ensure a safe and enjoyable experience. Camp only at designated sites. Reservations can be made at www.campwithme.com. Respect the quiet hours in camping areas between 10:00 p.m. and 7:00 a.m. Generators are permitted between 8:00 a.m. and 8:00 p.m., as long as they do not disrupt the tranquility of other visitors. Start fires only in designated areas with fire pits or grills. Avoid cutting live vegetation. Keep pets leashed, attended, and under control at all times. Carry out all trash and dispose of it properly to keep the park clean and protect the environment. Refrain from discharging firearms within 300 feet of picnic areas, camping areas, parking areas, marked hiking trails, or other developed areas. Loaded firearms are not permitted at campsites or on hiking trails for the safety of all visitors. If you plan to fish, ensure you have a valid fishing license and adhere to the state's open water fishing regulations. Consider using lead-free sinkers and jigs to prevent metal poisoning of wildlife. Visit www.maine.gov/ifw/ for more information. If you plan to hike the entire 3-mile trail system, it is highly recommended to start by ascending the South Peak Trail and then continue on to the North Peak Trail in a clockwise direction. Going up the South Peak Trail is much easier than hiking down it. During the winter season, the hiking trails are open for snowshoeing unless otherwise indicated. North Peak Trail (moderate to difficult, 0.6 miles): This trail offers scenic views as it takes you through upland hardwoods and conifers. It starts at the day use parking area. Notch Trail (moderate, 0.25 miles): This trail showcases the natural beauty of the park as it follows an intermittent brook that originates from the mountain top and flows through a gorge. You can access it near the start of the South Peak Trail or along the Ridge Trail, providing a safer and easier route on or off the mountain. Ridge Trail (easy, 1 mile): This trail meanders along the ridge between the North and South Peaks, offering diverse vegetation on the forest floor. You can access it from either the North or South Peak Trails. QuaQuaJo Nature Trail (easy, 0.5 miles): This loop trail takes you through a mature forest with flowing springs and a wide variety of trees, plants, birds, and animals. You can access it from the south end of the parking lot or via the campground road. South Peak Trail (difficult/strenuous, 0.4 miles): This trail presents a steep and rugged but interesting climb. It follows a forested path before reaching a rocky outcrop at the peak. You can access it from the campground. Aroostook State Park offers 15 miles of groomed cross-country ski trails with grooved double set tracks suitable for skiers of all skill levels. It is important to stay on the designated trails and respect the private property owners who have allowed access to their land for the trail system. At the intersection of the Maze and Red Pine Trails, there is a warming hut available for skiers. Beech Trail (novice, 0.2 miles): This trail runs from the Novice Trail to the campground, where the Sheep and Quaggy Jo Mt. Trails begin. Cedar Trail (intermediate, 0.5 miles): The Cedar Trail connects with the Maze, Novice, and Sheep Trails. It winds through a cedar swamp, fields, and a stand of new growth hardwoods. Lookout Trail (advanced, 0.5 miles): This ungroomed trail starts from and returns to the south side of the Quaggy Jo Mountain Trail as an up-and-back trail. It traverses scenic upland hardwood and evergreen forests. Maple Trail (advanced, 2 miles): The Maple Trail loops off the south end of the Quaggy Jo Mountain Trail. It offers rolling hills and turns. Maze Trail (novice, 1 mile): This trail begins from an intersection on the Novice Trail and winds through a tree plantation and a forest management area on a neighboring farm. Novice Trail (novice, 1 mile): Starting at the south end of the parking lot, the Novice Trail meanders through a cedar swamp, connecting the Sheep, Cedar, and Maze Trails. Old Beacon Trail (intermediate, 0.5 miles): This trail leads from the Quaggy Jo Mountain Trail across rolling terrain to the former site of an aviation beacon. It provides an outstanding westerly view of the countryside. Quaggy Jo Mountain Trail (advanced, 4 miles): The Quaggy Jo Mountain Trail starts at campground site #18, is for one-way traffic, and returns to the campground at the Kitchen Shelter. It follows the route of the South Peak Nature Trail for a short distance before turning to circle Quaggy Jo Mountain. This trail offers the widest variety of terrain among all the trails in the park. Red Pine Trail (novice, 0.2 miles): Branching off the Maze Trail, the Red Pine Trail winds through a managed red pine plantation and ends in a farm field with a nice view of Quaggy Jo Mountain and the surrounding area. Sheep Trail (intermediate, 1.5 miles): The Sheep Trail starts near campground site #21 and winds through a hardwood forest, passing the edge of an old sheep farm. To return, you can follow the route of the Novice Trail. Aroostook State Park serves as an excellent starting point for exploring the captivating North Maine Woods, the breathtaking Allagash Wilderness Waterway, and the neighboring Canadian provinces of New Brunswick and Quebec. The Allagash Wilderness Waterway is a federally designated Wild and Scenic River that spans 92 miles, offering a pristine river corridor for canoe enthusiasts and nature lovers. For more information, visit www.maine.gov/allagash. Deboullie Public Lands provide an opportunity for remote camping and fishing in serene trout ponds, surrounded by rugged mountains and encompassing an expansive area of 21,871 acres. Situated just 30 miles from the Canadian border, it offers a truly captivating wilderness experience. Learn more at www.maine.gov/deboullie. Fort Kent Block House holds historical significance as a State Historic Site. Originally constructed in 1839 during the "Aroostook War" to secure Maine's claim to the northern forest, it stands as a testament to the region's past. Located off U.S. Route #1 / West Main Street in Fort Kent, it offers a glimpse into the area's rich history. Find out more at www.maine.gov/fortkent. Scopan Public Lands boast some of the most rugged and captivating terrain in the vicinity. This area encompasses the majestic 1,400-foot Scopan Mountain, 9.5 miles of picturesque shoreline along Scopan Lake, as well as low hills, wetlands, brooks, and a charming small pond. To explore this remarkable landscape, visit www.maine.gov/scopan.

NOTES:

PASSPORT STAMPS

BAXTER STATE PARK

COUNTY: PISCATAQUIS	ESTABLISHED: 1930	AREA (AC/HA): 209,644 / 84,839
DATE VISITED:	LODGING:	WHO I WENT WITH:

WEATHER: ☀☐ ☁☐ ☷☐ ❄☐ ⛆☐ ☁☐   SPRING ☐ SUMMER ☐ FALL ☐ WINTER ☐

FEE(S):	RATING: ☆ ☆ ☆ ☆ ☆	WILL I RETURN? YES / NO

Percival P. Baxter, who served as the governor of Maine from 1921 to 1924, had a deep appreciation for the Maine wilderness and enjoyed fishing and vacationing in the woods since childhood. His love for the land and its wildlife played a vital role in his vision of creating a park for the people of Maine. In 1930, he took the first step towards realizing his dream by purchasing nearly 6,000 acres of land, including Katahdin, the highest peak in Maine. The following year, in 1931, Baxter officially donated the parcel of land to the State of Maine with the condition that it be forever preserved as a wild and untouched area. Over the years, Governor Baxter continued to acquire additional lands, carefully piecing together his park through various transactions. His final purchase was made in 1962, further expanding the park's size. Currently, the park encompasses a total of 209,644 acres, with approximately 75% of the land (156,874 acres) managed as a wildlife sanctuary. In the northwest corner of the park, 29,537 acres (around 14% of the park) have been designated by Governor Baxter as the Scientific Forest Management Area. Additionally, about 25% of the park (52,628 acres) is open for hunting and trapping, with the exception that moose hunting is prohibited within the park boundaries. In a display of remarkable generosity and forward-thinking, Percival P. Baxter established a trust worth nearly 7 million dollars to ensure the ongoing maintenance of the park, free from the need to rely on taxpayer funds from the general account of the state of Maine. Furthermore, Baxter specified that the governance and management of the park would rest solely in the hands of three public officials: the Commissioner of Maine Inland Fisheries and Wildlife, the Director of the Maine State Forest Service, and the Attorney General. Together, these individuals form the Baxter State Park Authority, entrusted with the responsibility of safeguarding the park's natural resources and upholding the conditions outlined in Governor Baxter's Deeds of Trust. To ensure a collaborative and well-rounded approach to park stewardship, park managers closely collaborate with the BSP Advisory, a committee consisting of 15 dedicated citizens. This committee is committed to examining various issues related to the park and providing support in the responsible management of the Authority's duties. Within the Park, there exists a remarkable array of natural features, including over 40 peaks and ridges in addition to Katahdin. These diverse landscapes offer ample opportunities for exploration, with a trail system spanning more than 215 miles. These trails are highly popular among hikers, mountain climbers, and nature enthusiasts who are drawn to the Park's beauty. As a result of its exceptional offerings, the Park has become a premier destination for outdoor enthusiasts throughout the year. The summer months witness an influx of approximately 60,000 visitors to the Park, with some staying for extended periods while others enjoy a day trip. Baxter State Park is situated in the Northern Forest Region of the American Continent, where it experiences the characteristic cool and moist climate of this area. The peak of summer temperatures and conditions within the Park is observed during the months of July and August. Snowfall, which lasts from mid to late November until April, blankets the Park during the winter season. It's important to note that weather in Baxter State Park is characterized by its variability. Snowfall can occur in any month of the year, and temperatures have a tendency to fluctuate widely around the average. Visitors to the Park should be prepared for these changes and the potential for unexpected weather conditions throughout the year. Baxter State Park, in its present form, began taking shape approximately 12,000 years ago when the Laurentide ice sheet melted and retreated from New England. At that time, even Katahdin was covered by glacial ice. Over the next 1,000 years, the land that would eventually become the Park transitioned into a tundra ecosystem, and evidence of early human inhabitants can be found. As the following millennium unfolded, forests gradually emerged, transforming the landscape: The development of the first forests in northern New England had a significant impact on the Paleo-Indian culture. The boreal forests of spruce and fir, which provide limited herbaceous vegetation, were not suitable for sustaining herbivores like caribou. As a result, some large herbivores, including musk ox and caribou, gradually moved away from the region and ventured further north. Many other species became extinct, as they could no longer find sufficient food resources. Over the next 8,000 years, as the climate gradually warmed, the forests of northern Maine evolved from the boreal forests found farther north to the "Acadian" forest dominated by spruce and fir. This type of forest thrives in poorly or moderately drained soils, typically on compressed glacial till or areas with shallow soil over bedrock. Within the Park, there are several mountain ranges, with two prominent clusters standing out: the peaks surrounding the Katahdin massif and the cluster of peaks in the northern part known as the Traveler Range. The mountains in the southern region of the Park are characterized by the ruggedness of pink and white Katahdin granite. Moving towards the north, the Traveler Range is predominantly composed of Rhyolite, which exhibits distinctive columnar jointing in various areas. Additionally, certain locations in the northern part of the Park feature sedimentary rock formations. Glacial remnants can be observed extensively throughout the Park, including kettle ponds, eskers, moraines, and erratics. Notable glacial features include the Knife Edge arête and the glacial cirques of Katahdin, as well as the impressive U-shaped valley that runs from north to south, spanning from the Travelers to South Turner. The landscape of Baxter State Park is enhanced by a diverse range of features, including mountains, ponds, lakes, streams, waterfalls, and bogs, creating a captivating and varied environment. Notable waterfalls like Katahdin Stream Falls, Big and Little Niagara Falls, and the secluded Green Falls are cherished by visitors. Two significant streams, Nesowadnehunk Stream and Wassataquoik Stream, add to the park's natural charm. Numerous ponds such as Kidney Pond, Daicey Pond, Grassy Pond, Rocky Pond, and the Fowler Ponds offer excellent fishing opportunities and picturesque settings for canoeing amidst the scenic northern woods. The park is also home to several bogs, which host unique plant species, birds, and wildlife. The forested areas of the park teem with a diverse array of wildlife, including moose, deer, bear, otter, mink, marten, fisher, weasel, coyote, bobcat, beaver, muskrat, raccoon, woodchucks, snowshoe hare, squirrels, chipmunks, flying squirrels, mice, and voles. Bird enthusiasts will be delighted by the variety of habitats found in the park, attracting wood warblers, thrushes, flycatchers, game birds, owls, hawks, ducks, and other wetland birds. Amphibians and reptiles, representative of freshwater habitats in northern New England, provide engaging encounters for young campers. The plant life within the park is as diverse as its terrain and wildlife. However, the most popular plants among summer visitors are undoubtedly the blueberries, raspberries, and blackberries. Unlike parks designed for car access and scenic viewpoints along roads, Baxter State Park's features and diversity are best explored on foot. The park maintains over 200 miles of trails, ranging from well-traveled boardwalks around Sandy Stream Pond to remote and less frequented trails like Freezeout and rugged Northwest Basin Trail. There are moderate trails around ponds, pleasant paths leading to waterfalls, and challenging routes strewn with boulders for those seeking to conquer the park's mountains. It's important to note that pets are not allowed in the park. The park offers several picnic areas. The Abol Pond Shelter is situated at the western edge of Abol Pond, offering visitors the chance to enjoy swimming and canoeing activities. Togue Pond Beach, located just a few hundred feet from the Park's Visitor Center, is the most popular spot within Baxter State Park for day-use picnicking and swimming. For those looking to combine a hike with a meal, the park provides two hike-in Picnic Shelters: The Katahdin Lake Shelter is accessed via a 3.2-mile hike from the Avalanche Field trailhead on the Roaring Brook Road. It offers excellent opportunities for swimming and fishing in Katahdin Lake. Visitors can also rent canoes from the nearby canoe site (remember to request a key at either Togue Pond Gatehouse or Roaring Brook Campground). The Dwelley Pond Shelter is another option and offers great opportunities for wildlife viewing. A canoe is available for rental at this shelter as well (remember to request a key at either Togue Pond Gatehouse, Matagamon Gatehouse, Trout Brook Farm, or Nesowadnehunk Campground). Canoes and kayaks can be rented at various pondside campgrounds within the Park and most backcountry ponds that have trail access. Additionally, most backcountry lean-tos located by a lake or pond have a designated canoe available for campers staying at the site. While opportunities for whitewater canoeing in the Park are limited, Webster Stream offers some options. It features class 1, 2, and 3 waters, including a class 5 drop at Grand Pitch. The water levels in Webster Stream are influenced by rain events and changes in the dam gates upstream at Telos Dam. Due to the remote nature of Webster Stream, canoeing on this stream is restricted to parties that have reserved at least one campsite in the Park. Park policy requires parties canoeing Webster Stream to spend the previous night at Webster Outlet or another site on Webster Lake. This ensures enough time to paddle the 9-mile stream and reach another campsite on Matagamon Lake or exit the Park via Trout Brook Farm. In most Park ponds, the use of motors is not permitted. However, motors are allowed on Matagamon, Webster, and Nesowadnehunk Lakes. For Upper and Lower Togue Pond, motors with 10 HP or less are permitted. Fishing is a popular activity among Park visitors. For safety reasons, children aged 10 and under are required to wear a Type I, II, or III personal flotation device (PFD) in all watercraft. If you need to purchase a fishing license, State of Maine fishing licenses are available for sale at Matagamon Gatehouse, the Visitor Center, and all Ranger Stations. Maine residents under 16 years old and nonresidents under 12 years old may fish without a license. Hunting and trapping are allowed in approximately 25% of the Park, with some restrictions. Moose hunting and hunting over bait are not permitted. The specific areas where hunting is allowed are outlined in the Park's rules. These areas include the entire Scientific Forest Management Area (SFMA), which consists of about 1,000 acres surrounding Upper and Lower Togue Pond, acquired by the Park Authority in 1993, and over 2,000 acres north of the West Branch of the Penobscot River, acquired by the Baxter State Park Authority in 1997. The majority of hunting activities occur in the Park's Scientific Forest Management Area (SFMA), which is located in the northwest corner of the Park. Hunters can access the SFMA via the Telos Road and Useless Roads (private), and they will have access to the Wadleigh Mountain Road east to the junction with the Frost Pond Road. From the Matagamon gate, hunters have access to a portion of the SFMA road system between the Lynx Gate and the Frost Pond Gate. Park Gatehouses are operational throughout the main hunting season until the end of November. Cycling is allowed on two specific routes in the Park: the Park Tote Road and the Dwelley Pond Trail. Additionally, cycling is permitted on parts of the SFMA road system that are not currently used for logging operations. During the winter months, fat biking is allowed on the Abol Stream trail and the Park Tote Road. The park provides a unique opportunity for climbers seeking remote and demanding technical climbing experiences in New England. Climbers will discover a wide range of climbing options to test their skills, including bouldering and multi-pitch climbs. The majority of climbing routes on Katahdin can be accessed from Chimney Pond, which requires a 3.3-mile hike from Roaring Brook Campgrounds. The duration of the approaches to these climbs can vary from 30 minutes to 2 hours. To ensure a smooth climb for routes such as the Armadillo, Flat Iron, and Pamola 4, it is recommended to depart from Chimney Pond no later than 8:00 am. The interpretive programs offered in Baxter State Park are designed to enhance your knowledge of the park's natural and cultural history. Rangers lead various programs, including Family Programs, Evening Campground Programs, and Walk with a Ranger programs. The park is open for day use from 6:00 am to 10:00 pm. It is mandatory to check-in at the gate no later than 8:30 pm on the first night of your camping stay. Quiet hours in the park are observed from 9:00 pm to 7:00 am. Most campgrounds in Baxter State Park are open from May 15th onwards. To accommodate visitors, Baxter State Park operates eight roadside campgrounds and two backcountry campgrounds. Additionally, there are numerous individual backcountry sites available for backpackers, providing a range of options for those seeking an immersive outdoor experience. Katahdin Stream Campground, established in 1939, is a well-known and beloved destination for families. It offers a variety of recreational opportunities, including convenient access to the majestic Mount Katahdin through the renowned Appalachian Trail. Additionally, the campground provides easy entry to a multitude of streams and ponds in the scenic Kidney and Daicey area, allowing visitors to explore and enjoy the natural beauty of the region. Situated approximately 26 miles from Millinocket, Katahdin Stream Campground offers a range of accommodation options to suit different preferences. It features 12 lean-tos and 9 tent sites. Furthermore, the campground includes 3 group sites, accommodating larger gatherings of 12, 13, and 25 people respectively. Abol Campground is situated in a beautiful northern hardwood forest, close to the base of Abol Slide. It holds the distinction of being the nearest campground to Togue Pond Gate and serves as a convenient trailhead for hiking to Katahdin. The campground is located approximately 24 miles from Millinocket and offers 12 lean-tos and 9 tent sites. Roaring Brook Campground is one of the busiest campgrounds in the Park, mainly due to its popularity as a trailhead for hiking to Chimney Pond and Katahdin. It offers convenient access to the Avalanche Field trailhead for Martin Ponds, as well as the Katahdin Lake day use shelter, which provides canoes for day use. Additionally, the campground is close to the Katahdin Lake Wilderness Camps. The campground is located approximately 26 miles from Millinocket and offers 9 lean-tos, 10 tent sites, and a bunkhouse that can accommodate up to 10 people. Daicey Pond Campground is a remote and rustic wilderness campground that immerses you in the natural surroundings. It offers 10 cabins of varied design and size. To ensure a comfortable stay, it is important to come prepared with essential items. You will need to bring your own sleeping bag or sheets, blankets, and pillows. As there are no on-site stores within Baxter Park, it is crucial to bring all the necessary meal supplies with you. Groceries can be obtained in nearby towns such as Millinocket, which is located 20 miles from the Togue Pond gate at the south entrance, or Patten, situated 24 miles from the Matagamon gate at the north entrance. In addition to bedding and meal supplies, it is advisable to bring dishes, cooking utensils, a gas stove for cooking meals, basins for washing dishes and personal items, a bucket for carrying water from the pond, a cooler for storing perishable food items, gas lanterns for lighting, towels for personal use, and any other items that would contribute to the comfort and convenience of you and your family during your stay at the campground. Kidney Pond Campground is a remote and rustic wilderness campground. There are 12 cabins of varied design and size available, with one cabin requiring a 1-mile canoe or hike-in. The cabins are equipped with outdoor fireplaces for cooking and picnic tables. Most cabins have communal fireplaces, but only three cabins have their own fire rings. Dishes, cooking utensils, a gas stove for cooking, basins for washing dishes and personal hygiene, a bucket to carry water from the pond, a cooler, gas lanterns, towels, bedding, and any other items that would make your stay more comfortable should be brought with you. Nesowadnehunk is the most secluded campground along the Park's roadside, offering a sense of remoteness. It conveniently grants access to Ledge Falls, a popular swimming spot during hot summer days. This campground serves as a starting point for the Wassataquoik Lake Trail, leading to

Russell Pond, and also provides opportunities for day hikes to Doubletop Mountain. In 2005-2008, Nesowadnehunk Field Campground underwent a restructure where all lean-tos were relocated to the former group area field. The bridge over Nesowadnehunk Stream is now open for foot traffic only and provides access to several walk-in tent sites. Nesowadnehunk is situated approximately 35 miles away from Millinocket. It offers 11 lean-tos, 9 tent sites, and an 8-person bunkhouse for accommodation. South Branch Pond is the largest campground in the Park and has gained popularity among families who come back year after year. It offers a variety of recreational opportunities, including access to local ponds in the Fowler region and the option for day hikes on South Branch Mountain, North Traveler, and the challenging Traveler Loop Trail. The campground's trailhead also serves as an entry point to Russell Pond Campground via the Pogy Notch Trail. Located approximately 33.5 miles west of Patten, South Branch Pond campground features 12 lean-tos, 21 tent sites, and a bunkhouse with a capacity of 8 people. Trout Brook Farm is a serene campground within the Park, offering a peaceful atmosphere for visitors. It serves as an excellent starting point for exploring Matagamon Lake and engaging in backcountry hiking and camping adventures in the northern region of the Park. Located approximately 26.5 miles west of Patten, Trout Brook Farm features a range of accommodation options. It includes 1 lean-to, which requires a short 0.3-mile walk to reach, providing a more secluded experience. Additionally, there are 14 tent sites available for individual campers or small groups. For larger groups, the campground offers 4 group sites. Site 1 can accommodate up to 8 people, while sites 2, 3, and 4 have a capacity of 14 individuals each. Chimney Pond, established in 1938, is a highly sought-after campground within Baxter State Park and one of the two backcountry campgrounds available in the park. It holds immense popularity among visitors. Chimney Pond serves as a starting point for day hikes to all the peaks of Katahdin and also provides access to Russell Pond Campground through Davis Pond and the Northwest Basin Trail. It is important to note that there is an established cut-off time for hikers leaving to venture into Chimney Pond, which is set at 5:00 p.m. During the fall season, as daylight hours shorten, the posted cut-off time may vary and be earlier. It is recommended to verify these specific cut-off times with the reservation office and plan your activities accordingly. To preserve the environment and prevent further degradation, open fires are prohibited in the area. Access to Chimney Pond is available via a 3.3-mile trail starting from Roaring Brook. The campground offers 9 lean-tos for overnight stays, providing shelter and a rustic camping experience. Additionally, there is a bunkhouse available with a capacity of 10 people, offering a communal accommodation option. Russell Pond, located deep within Baxter State Park, is renowned as the most remote campground in the park and one of the two backcountry campgrounds available. It offers a truly secluded and immersive wilderness experience. Russell Pond is particularly attractive to fishing enthusiasts, as it provides excellent fishing opportunities in nearby ponds. Additionally, it serves as a gateway to explore Wassataquoik Stream, Wassataquoik Lake, and several popular backcountry campsites in the vicinity. To reach Russell Pond, hikers can choose between two main routes. They can embark on a backpacking journey of either 7.2 or 7.6 miles starting from Roaring Brook, or opt for a longer 9.6-mile hike from South Branch Pond. It's important to note that there is an established cutoff time for departing to hike towards Russell Pond, which is set at 2:00 p.m. As daylight hours shorten in the fall, posted cut-off time is earlier. Visitors should verify these cut-off times with the reservation office and make your plans accordingly. While making your way to Russell Pond, you should be aware that there are no bridges over Wassataquoik Stream. Crossing involves rock hopping and wading through the stream. Please note that trail access may be temporarily closed from Roaring Brook during periods of high water or challenging conditions. Upon reaching Russell Pond, you will find a total of 5 lean-tos available for overnight stays, providing basic shelter and rustic accommodation options. Additionally, there are 3 tent sites designated for those preferring to set up their own tents. For larger groups, there is an 8-person bunkhouse available, offering a communal sleeping arrangement. Katahdin Lake is under private ownership and operates through a lease agreement with the Baxter State Park Authority. To access the campsites at Katahdin Lake, visitors must embark on a scenic 3.3-mile hike starting from the Avalanche Field trailhead, which is located on the Roaring Brook Road within the boundaries of Baxter State Park. There is no potable water available within the park. It is important to note that all water sources in the park should be treated with caution, as they may not be safe for consumption. Therefore, it is necessary to treat all water before use to ensure its safety. Please be aware that this is a wilderness area, and there are no facilities to purchase cooking or sleeping supplies within the park. Additionally, there are no shower facilities available; only outhouses are provided. The park's trail system spans more than 215 miles. The Abol trail is the quickest way to reach Baxter Peak starting from a trailhead accessible by road. Previously, the trail followed the prominent Abol Slide, but it was relocated in 2015 due to safety concerns caused by soil and rock movement on the slide. The new trail now follows the ridge to the west of the slide, offering a steady and steep ascent with impressive views. It's important to note that water sources become scarce after the first mile, and the trail becomes completely exposed after 2.5 miles. Therefore, it is advisable to start early, especially on warm days. Once you reach the Tableland, you will join the Hunt trail (part of the Appalachian Trail) for the final mile to Baxter Peak. The Hunt trail is highly favored among hikers seeking to reach the summit of Katahdin. Its popularity stems from the remarkable attractions found along the trail, including the scenic Katahdin Stream Falls, the impressive Boulders on Hunt Spur, the traverse of the Tableland, and the expansive panoramic views in every direction. It is worth noting that approximately 2.4 miles of the trail extends above the tree line, providing a unique and breathtaking experience for hikers. The Helon Taylor trail offers hikers a direct path from the Roaring Brook trailhead to reach the Knife Edge trail at Pamola Peak. However, it is important to note that this trail is highly exposed, meaning that hikers are fully exposed to the elements and the terrain. As a result, it is strongly advised not to attempt this hike in unfavorable weather conditions. The Cathedral trail is the quickest route from Chimney Pond to reach Baxter Peak. In order to reach the peak, the trail includes a section on the Saddle

Trail for an additional 0.2 miles. The Cathedral trail involves a challenging ascent, as it climbs steeply over three prominent rock buttresses. Most of the climbing on this trail is above the tree line, offering expansive views. It's important to note that there are no water sources along the trail, so hikers should ensure they have an adequate water supply before starting the hike. The Saddle trail offers a more gradual ascent compared to other trails. Hikers will reach Saddle Brook approximately 0.8 miles from the Chimney Pond campground, which is the last reliable water source along the trail. The most challenging section of the trail is a 0.2-mile slide just before reaching the Tableland. Hikers should be prepared for difficult footing, including loose stones and gravel in this particular section of the trail. The Knife Edge trail is a challenging and exposed route, and it has been the site of fatalities and serious injuries during attempts in bad weather conditions and high winds. Once you start traversing the ridge, it is strongly advised not to deviate from the path. It is not recommended to hike the Knife Edge trail in its entirety and then return due to its difficulty and the additional time it adds to the hike. The one-way journey on the trail typically takes approximately 1 to 1½ hours. The trail can be accessed from the Roaring Brook Campground. If you choose to hike it from the Hunt or Abol Trails, you will end up at Roaring Brook Campground, which is located approximately an hour away by road from your vehicle on the other side of the mountain. Please note that there is no water available along this trail. The Hamlin Ridge trail is a scenic and expansive ridge that provides breathtaking views. It starts on the North Basin Trail, approximately 0.7 miles away from Chimney Pond Campground. From there, it follows a lengthy ridge leading to Hamlin Peak and continues its descent to Caribou Spring, where it meets the Northwest Basin Trail junction. It's important to note that this trail does not provide direct access to Baxter Peak. However, you have the option to embark on a 4.5-mile loop by hiking to Hamlin Peak and then returning via the Northwest Basin Trail, which connects back to the Saddle Trail and ultimately descends to Chimney Pond Campground. The Chimney Pond trail leads you directly to the Chimney Pond Campground. After the initial 0.1 mile, the Helon Taylor trail veers off from the Chimney Pond Trail. The hike along the Chimney Pond Trail begins with a gradual incline and gradually becomes a moderately challenging hike. There are some steep sections along the trail, and the majority of the path is covered with rocks. You will find ample water sources available throughout this trail. The Traveler Loop is a combination of four trails that offers an extended hike spanning over 10 miles. It encompasses three major peaks and includes sections above the treeline, providing breathtaking views. The trailhead for the Traveler Loop is located at South Branch Pond Campground. To reach this campground, it is best to enter through the Matagamon Gate at the northeast corner of the Park. No parking reservations are required for this trailhead. The Traveler Loop begins with the Pogy Notch Trail, covering a distance of 1.5 miles. It then continues onto the Center Ridge Trail for 2.1 miles, followed by the Traveler Trail for 3.7 miles, and finally concludes with the North Traveler Trail for 2.6 miles. Along this loop, hikers will summit three peaks: Peak of the Ridges, The Traveler, and North Traveler Mountain. The total elevation gain for this hike is 3,700 feet, just 400 feet less than what is required for a Katahdin hike on the Hunt Trail. The Traveler Loop can be hiked in either direction, but it is recommended to traverse the loop in a counter-clockwise direction, ascending the Center Ridge Trail starting from Upper South Branch Pond. It's important to note that water sources become scarce or non-existent along the Traveler Loop after leaving the Pogy Notch Trail near Upper South Branch Pond. Therefore, it is advised that hikers carry at least 2 quarts of water per person, and even more on hot days. This hike is demanding and strenuous, with extended exposure above the treeline. Hikers should be mindful of changing weather conditions and be prepared for a challenging yet rewarding adventure.

NOTES:

PASSPORT STAMPS

BIRCH POINT STATE PARK

COUNTY: KNOX   **ESTABLISHED:** 1999   **AREA (AC/HA):** 62 / 25

DATE VISITED: **LODGING:**   **WHO I WENT WITH:**

WEATHER: ☀☐ ⛅☐ 🌧☐ ❄☐ ⛈☐ 🌫☐   SPRING ☐ SUMMER ☐ FALL ☐ WINTER ☐

FEE(S):   **RATING:** ☆ ☆ ☆ ☆ ☆   **WILL I RETURN?** YES / NO

Birch Point State Park is an ideal destination for those seeking tranquility and serenity. The park is open from Memorial Day to Labor Day, from 9:00 a.m. until sunset every day, unless there are different instructions at the gate. There is a fee for entry, and only cash or check payments are accepted; credit cards are not allowed. If you want to visit the park outside the designated season, you can park your vehicle outside the gate without blocking it and walk in during the same hours. Please remember to put the admission fee in the self-service collection box. It's important to note that the park facilities are closed during the off season. Despite being smaller and less historically significant than other parks, this particular park compensates for it with its uncomplicated charm and natural beauty. Indulge in the picturesque vistas of Penobscot Bay as you partake in a relaxing picnic or fishing excursion. The park offers a charming, crescent-shaped sandy beach where you can enjoy a swim in calm waters. The beach is wide and the water is shallow. The wooded area has shaded picnic tables or you can sit on the rocks. It's important to note that there are no lifeguards on duty, so swimmers should exercise caution. In addition to these water activities, the park also provides opportunities for observing the local wildlife. There are many trails for hiking around the property, some in the woods and others along the shore. On either end of the beach, you can follow short paths that lead to stunning secluded spots, smooth bedrock formations, and areas adorned with cobblestones and pebbles. There are quiet spots with secluded barbecue stands. Toilets are available in the park.

NOTES:

PASSPORT STAMPS

BRADBURY MOUNTAIN STATE PARK

COUNTY: CUMBERLAND	ESTABLISHED: 1939	AREA (AC/HA): 800 / 323

DATE VISITED:	LODGING:	WHO I WENT WITH:

WEATHER: ☀☐ ☁☐ 🌧☐ ❄☐ ⚡☐ 🌊☐   SPRING ☐ SUMMER ☐ FALL ☐ WINTER ☐

FEE(S):	RATING: ☆ ☆ ☆ ☆ ☆	WILL I RETURN? YES / NO

Bradbury Mountain State Park offers a delightful setting for spending a day or afternoon, where you can explore various trails, or admire the breathtaking view from the summit. Conveniently located on Route 9, roughly halfway between Portland and Lewiston-Auburn, this park attracts visitors who appreciate activities such as picnicking, hiking, and camping across its expansive 800-acre wooded terrain. At the park, visitors can also enjoy such activities and experiences as birdwatching, cross-country skiing, hunting, self-guided trail exploration, snowshoeing, and observing wildlife.What sets Bradbury Mountain apart is its unique offering of shared-use trails, accommodating horseback riders, mountain bikers, and snowmobilers, making it the only state park in southern Maine with such diverse recreational options. For those interested, snowshoe rentals are available. One of the park's most remarkable natural features is Bradbury Mountain itself, which was sculpted by ancient glaciers. Prior to the arrival of the first European settlers, the Wabanakis, a Native American tribe, would camp on the mountain during their journeys to the nearby coast. In the early 1800s, the Cotton family cultivated grapes on terraces that can still be seen on the mountain today. As a means to contain wandering cattle, sheep, and pigs, the early settlers constructed a cattle pound, which remains standing near the Northern Loop Trail on Route 9. In the vicinity of the ball field, visitors can also observe the remnants of feldspar mining sites from the 1920s, where the mineral was extracted for the production of crockery and china. Bradbury Mountain was acquired from the Federal Government in 1939 and became one of the original five state parks. During the 1940s, it even offered downhill skiing facilities with a rope tow. In the 1990s, the park expanded by an additional 250 acres, made possible through the generosity of the Spiegel family, funding from the Lands for Maine's Future Fund, and the dedicated efforts of numerous individuals. These groups continue to work towards further expanding the park, with the eventual goal of connecting it to the Pineland Public Land parcel in New Gloucester. The park's forest is now home to a diverse array of plant and animal species, creating a vibrant ecosystem. Springtime, particularly from mid-March to mid-May, is an ideal period for witnessing the hawk migration spectacle. During this time, the park hosts the annual Hawk Watch, an initiative established in 2007 by Jeannette and Derek Lovitch. The hawk count conducted during this event generates valuable quantitative data, shedding light on the magnitude and duration of the northbound raptor flight over Bradbury Mountain State Park. The park is accessible throughout the year, from 9:00 a.m. until sunset every day, unless there are specific instructions posted at the gate. Even during the off-season when the park is closed, visitors can still enjoy it by parking their vehicles outside the gate without obstructing it, and walking in during the same hours of operation. However, it's important to note that the park's facilities are closed during the off-season. A fee is required for entry into the park, and it is collected year-round either by the park staff at the entry booth or through a self-service station. The park offers various services and facilities to enhance visitors' experiences, including: group picnic shelter, picnic area, playground, and showers. The park offers year-round trail activities. East Side Trails include: The Fox East Trail is a 1.4-mile trail that offers a moderate to intermediate level of difficulty for most activities. However, it is considered a difficult and challenging trail for horseback riding. The trail is known for its technical sections and narrow pathway. Similarly, the Fox West Trail spans 1.2 miles and is also classified as moderate to intermediate for most activities. However, it presents a challenging and difficult terrain for horseback riding. The trail features technical sections and a narrow pathway. For those looking for a longer trail, the Ginn Trail extends for 2.6 miles. It is considered moderate to intermediate for most activities, but it poses a challenging and most difficult route for horseback riding. The trail offers technical sections and a narrow pathway. The Knight Woods Trail is a 1.1-mile trail that offers an easy and wide pathway with a slight incline. It is suitable for all activities and provides a pleasant hiking experience. The Lanzo Trail extends for 1.6 miles and is classified as moderate to intermediate for most activities. However, it becomes a challenging and most difficult trail for horseback riding. The trail is known for its technical sections and narrow pathway. The Link Trail covers a distance of 0.3 miles and offers an easy, flat, and wide pathway. In addition to serving as a trail for hikers, it also functions as a connector trail for snowmobiles. The "O" Trail is a 2.4-mile trail that poses a challenging and most difficult route for all activities. It is characterized by tight and demanding sections, providing a rigorous hiking experience. The Ragan Trail spans 0.7 miles and is considered moderate to intermediate for most activities. However, it presents a challenging and most difficult terrain for horseback riding. The trail features technical sections and a narrow pathway. Lastly, the Snowmobile Trail covers a distance of 1.5 miles and is classified as easy, although it includes some steep grades. This trail is primarily designed for snowmobiling but can also be used for other activities. West Side Trails include: The Bluff Trail is a short 0.2-mile trail that offers an easy and fairly flat pathway. It is primarily used for hiking and is marked with red blazes. The Boundary Trail spans 1.5 miles and is considered moderate to intermediate for hiking, but challenging and most difficult for all other activities. It features steep areas, sharp turns, and can become icy during winter. The trail is marked with orange blazes. The Northern Loop Trail covers a distance of 1.0 mile and is rated as easy for hiking, while being moderate to intermediate for all other activities. It gradually ascends to the summit of Mt. Blue and is marked with blue blazes. The Ski Trail is a 0.2-mile trail that is easy for hiking and moderate to intermediate for other activities. It features a short and gradual ascent and is marked with green blazes. The South Ridge Trail is a 0.5-mile hiking trail with a moderate to intermediate difficulty level. It includes a few steep areas and a ladder ascent. The trail is marked with red blazes. The Summit Trail spans 0.3 miles and is considered moderate to intermediate for hiking. It involves a short but steep ascent to the top of Bradbury Mountain and is marked with white blazes. The Terrace Trail is an easy 0.3-mile hiking trail that is wide and well-packed with a gradual ascent. It is marked with gray blazes. The Tote Road Trail covers a distance of 1.0 mile and is rated as easy, featuring a flat and wide looping pathway. It is marked with white blazes. Transporting firewood can inadvertently introduce harmful exotic insects and diseases that can severely impact forests. To prevent this threat, it is strongly advised not to move firewood from one location to another. Instead, it is recommended to purchase firewood from local sources to minimize the risk of spreading pests and diseases. Nearby attractions include Pineland Public Land, Wolfe's Neck Woods State Park, and Range Pond State Park.

NOTES:

PASSPORT STAMPS

CAMDEN HILLS STATE PARK

COUNTY: KNOX   ESTABLISHED: 1947   AREA (AC/HA): 5,710 / 2,310

DATE VISITED: LODGING: WHO I WENT WITH:

WEATHER: ☀□ ☁□ 🌦□ ❄□ 🌧□ 🌫□   SPRING □ SUMMER □ FALL □ WINTER □

FEE(S):   RATING: ☆☆☆☆☆   WILL I RETURN? YES / NO

Camden Hills State Park features a renowned spot known as the scenic vista atop Mt. Battie, where visitors can enjoy breathtaking panoramic views of Camden Harbor, Penobscot Bay, and the surrounding islands. On a clear day, it is even possible to see Cadillac Mountain at Acadia National Park. This stunning view is said to have served as inspiration for Edna St. Vincent Millay's poem "Renascence" and continues to captivate and amaze visitors to this day. The iconic Stone Tower, erected in 1921 as a memorial to the soldiers of World War I, stands proudly on the summit of Mt. Battie and serves as a prominent landmark for hikers. For those who prefer driving, the Mt. Battie Auto Road, constructed in the 1960s, leads directly to the tower. For generations, the allure of the Camden Hills has attracted individuals seeking sustenance from its abundant resources, establishing homes and engaging in recreational activities. People gather here to embrace the breathtaking vistas, feel the invigorating ocean winds, and draw inspiration from the majestic mountains that overlook the picturesque Penobscot Bay. The history of Mt. Battie is marked by significant transformations throughout the years. The Summit House hotel, originally constructed in 1897 by Columbus Buswell, was acquired by the conservation-oriented Mt. Battie Association in 1899. It underwent renovations and was renamed the Mt. Battie Clubhouse. Operating as a summer hotel, it welcomed the public until its demolition in October 1920. In 1921, the stone tower was erected and dedicated as a tribute to the brave soldiers from Camden who served their country during World War I. The Megunticook Cabin, now available for year-round reservations, has its own unique history. Initially established as part of a federal recreation area in the late 1930s, the Civilian Conservation Corps built it as a ski shelter. Originally called the Megunticook Ski Shelter, it served as a warm haven for skiers at the base of various ski slopes on the northern side of Mt. Megunticook. Skiers accessed the slopes by driving along plowed roads from Stevens Corner or by taking the Spring Brook truck road from US Route 1. Without any lifts available, skiers had to ascend to the summit after each run. The ski slopes remained open throughout the 1940s but eventually closed by the late 1950s, resulting in the gradual deterioration of the Ski Shelter. By the late 1980s, only a shell consisting of a roof supported by posts remained. The building was eventually demolished in the early 1990s. In 2005, park staff reconstructed the ski shelter using lumber harvested from the park's own property. Funding for the restoration project, including the rebuilding of the stone fireplaces and provision of building materials, was made possible through a grant from the MBNA Foundation. This recreational area is a popular destination all year round, offering a variety of outdoor activities. Visitors can engage in hiking, biking, cross-country skiing, snowshoeing, and camping. During spring, hikers are greeted with blooming wildflowers and the melodic songs of birds. Birdwatchers can enjoy the park's offerings throughout the year. It's important to be mindful of wildlife and their young, observing them from a safe distance. However, be prepared for the presence of black flies, ticks, and the browntail moth. During summer, hikers can take pleasure in the breathtaking vistas, diverse trails, and camping opportunities. Don't forget to get your Park Passport stamped and pick up the Jr. Ranger activity booklet, which will aid in exploring and learning more about the park while earning your badge. In autumn, visitors can admire the vibrant fall foliage either from the Mt. Battie Road or the trails. The optimal viewing time is usually from mid-September to mid-October. For foliage reports, you can visit mainefoliage.com. It's advisable to wear blaze orange attire during hunting season for safety. During winter, the park offers 7.6 miles of multi-use trails, providing ample opportunities for cross-country skiing. Keep in mind that these trails are also shared with snowmobiles. During winter, there are occasional visits from a Ski & Snowshoe Trailer, providing equipment and assistance for skiing and snowshoeing activities. The park offers 108 campsites, each equipped with a picnic table and fire pit. Some campsites have water and electric hook-ups available. Additionally, there is Wi-Fi access in the campground for a small fee. Campers have access to hot showers, flush toilets, and electricity and water facilities. The Megunticook Cabin, formerly known as the Ski Shelter, can be rented out. Vehicle parking for the cabin is located 2 miles away. A designated area for group camping is available, offering 5 sites exclusively for tent camping. For group picnics, there is a day-use Group Picnic Shelter with a picturesque ocean view that can be rented. The Megunticook Cabin is a popular choice for skiers, snowshoers, and snowmobile riders, and it is available for year-round reservations. Visitors can access the cabin by foot, bicycle, horseback, skis, or snowmobile. Reservations can be made up to a year in advance by contacting the park. The Megunticook Cabin is a rustic, insulated cabin measuring 20' x 40' and features a fieldstone fireplace. It does not have electricity or running water. An outdoor vault toilet is available on-site. The cabin provides sleeping accommodations for up to six people with bunk beds. Split and seasoned firewood can be purchased at the cabin for a fee. From December 15 to March 15, winter camping is available, but it is limited to primitive tent camping only. There are no water facilities, amenities, cleared campsites, or designated trails during this period. It is essential to have prior winter camping experience and be self-sufficient. Campsites can be accessed by snowshoeing or skiing, and some may require a short walk. Self-registration is required on-site, and you can find registration materials at the entry booth. Camping fees are applicable and can be paid in cash or by check at the self-registration station. For more information contact the park at (207) 236-0849. Camden Hills State Park offers a wide range of hiking trails, covering over 30 miles of scenic routes. The trails are marked with color symbols for easy navigation. Please note that during the winter, unless otherwise specified, the hiking trails are open for snowshoeing. Adam's Lookout Trail (easy, 0.3 miles) - This trail provides excellent views of Penobscot Bay and connects the Tablelands and Megunticook Trails. It takes approximately 10 minutes to complete. Bald Rock Trail (easy to moderate, 1.3 miles) - Leaving the Multi-use Trail at 1.3 miles, this trail offers stunning views of Penobscot Bay. Allow about 30 minutes for the hike. Bubba's Trail (easy to moderate, 0.8 miles) - Climbing through the woods, this trail leads to the Tablelands Trail. Plan for around 30 minutes to complete the hike. Cameron Mtn. Trail (easy, 1.9 miles) - Gradually ascending through old farmland and blueberry barren, this trail provides a pleasant hike. It takes approximately 1.5 hours. Carriage Road Trail (moderate, 0.8 miles) - Following an old carriage road, this trail leads to the summit of Mt. Battie. Allow about 45 minutes for the hike. Frohock Trail (moderate to strenuous, 1.9 miles) - This bike trail features a natural surface with rocks and roots, passing through oak and spruce forests over three mountains. Some sections have steep slopes, and it takes about 2 hours to complete. Jack Williams Trail (easy to moderate, 1.6 miles) - This trail offers views of lakes, hardwood forests, and rising cliffs, providing a picturesque experience. Allow around 1.5 hours. Maiden Cliff Trail (moderate, 1 mile) - With striking views from cliffs 800 feet above Megunticook Lake, this trail is worth the hike. Plan for approximately 1.5 hours. Megunticook Trail (moderate, 1 mile) - Featuring sweeping views of the ocean, lakes, and hills at Ocean Lookout, this trail is a scenic option. It takes about 1 hour to complete. Mt. Battie Trail (moderate to strenuous, 0.5 miles) - Reaching the summit, this trail offers a panoramic view, with some steep sections along the way. Allow around 45 minutes for the hike. Multi-use Trail (easy, 5 miles) - This pleasant forested route on the lower slopes of the mountains covers a distance of 5 miles. It takes approximately 3 hours to complete. Nature Trail (easy to moderate, 1.2 miles) - Gradually climbing the forested slopes, this trail leads to the Tablelands Trail. Plan for about 1 hour. Ridge Trail (moderate, 2.5 miles) - Covering Megunticook's ridge and wooded summit at 1,380 feet, this trail offers a rewarding hike. Allow around 2.5 hours. Scenic Trail (moderate, 0.8 miles) - At Millerite Ledges (920 feet), this trail provides fine views of mountains and lakes. It takes about 45 minutes to complete. Shoreline Trail (easy, 0.3 miles) - Following the scenic shoreline of Penobscot Bay, this trail offers a leisurely hike. Allow approximately 15 minutes. Sky Blue Trail (easy to moderate, 1.5 miles) - This trail winds its way through a blueberry barren, mature forest, and passes by a vernal pool. It is a pleasant hike and takes approximately 1.5 hours to complete. Slope Trail (moderate to strenuous, 1.5 miles) - Starting from the Megunticook Cabin, this trail ascends sharply to reach Megunticook's wooded summit. It offers a challenging hike and takes about 1.5 hours. Summer Bypass Trail (easy, 0.8 miles) - Crossing the northeast slope of Mt. Megunticook, this trail provides an alternate route to avoid low, wet areas on the Multi-use Trail. It is an easy hike and takes approximately 30 minutes. Tablelands Trail (moderate to strenuous, 1.5 miles) - Descending from Mt. Battie, this trail then rises to plateaus known as tablelands and passes by ledges before steadily climbing to Ocean Lookout at an elevation of 1,300 feet. Allow about 1.5 hours for the hike. Zeke's Trail (moderate, 1.3 miles) - Following a fairly steep old road, this trail includes a short spur leading to Zeke's Lookout. It is a moderately challenging hike and takes around 1 hour to complete. The Group Picnic Shelter in the park is a picturesque and historically significant venue suitable for various occasions, such as weddings, family reunions, or annual gatherings with friends. Reservations for the Group Picnic Shelter can be made starting at 9:00 a.m. on the first business day of February each year. To secure your reservation, please contact the park using the following numbers: for reservations in February through March, call: (207) 236-0849; for reservations in April through October, call: (207) 236-3109; for reservations in November through January, call: (207) 236-0849. Both young and old visitors can enhance their experience and actively engage with the park by obtaining a Junior Ranger booklet. By participating in this program, you not only have the opportunity to have fun, but also to earn a badge as a Junior Ranger. Camden Hills State Park is an excellent destination for exploring the Mid-coast region of Maine. There are several nearby attractions worth visiting. Birch Point State Park, situated in Owls Head, which provides access to the scenic shores of Penobscot Bay. The park features a beautiful crescent-shaped sandy beach where visitors can swim in the calm surf. Please note that there are no lifeguards on duty. Birch Point Beach Road, off Route 73 south of Owl's Head. The park operates from Memorial Day to October 1, and you can reach them at (207) 548-2882. Owls Head State Park, managed in partnership with the United States Coast Guard. This park grants visitors access to Owl's Head Light, a historic lighthouse dating back to 1852, perched on a granite promontory 100 feet above Penobscot Bay. Picnic tables and shoreline access are available at the park. It is located 4 miles off Route 73 on Lighthouse Road, Owl's Head. The park is open year-round and staffed by rangers from Camden Hills State Park. Warren Island State Park, designed for boating enthusiasts, is a tranquil spruce-covered island located off Lincolnville in Penobscot Bay. The park offers nine wooded campsites, three group campsites, three Adirondack shelters, a reservable group picnic shelter, fresh drinking water, and docking and mooring facilities on the northeast side of the island. It's important to note that there is no public ferry transportation available to the island. Warren Island State Park operates from Memorial Day to September 15.

NOTES:

PASSPORT STAMPS

COBSCOOK BAY STATE PARK

COUNTY: WASHINGTON	ESTABLISHED: 1964	AREA (AC/HA): 888 / 359

DATE VISITED:	LODGING:	WHO I WENT WITH:

WEATHER: ☼□ ☁□ ☔□ ❄□ ☂□ ☰□   SPRING □ SUMMER □ FALL □ WINTER □

FEE(S):	RATING: ☆ ☆ ☆ ☆ ☆	WILL I RETURN? YES / NO

Cobscook Bay State Park is a 422-acre park surrounded by the wildlife-rich waters of Cobscook Bay on three sides. It offers the perfect opportunity to observe birds and witness the impressive tides of the region. The name "Cobscook" comes from the Maliseet-Passamaquoddy tribe and refers to the "boiling tides" that are characteristic of this area. The tides here are much larger than the average tides along Maine's southern coast, with an average range of 24 feet and the ability to reach 28 feet. The park is an excellent choice for family camping and exploring the easternmost part of Maine. It provides 106 campsites for both tenting and RVs, many of which are located along Whiting Bay, a sheltered inlet within Cobscook Bay. The park also has a boat launch for experienced boaters who can handle the challenging conditions caused by the fast-moving tides and rapids. Cobscook Bay is a unique estuary with a narrow opening to the sea, a long and winding shoreline, and relatively few feeder streams and rivers. The nutrient-rich salt water that flows in from the Gulf of Maine promotes the growth of plankton, which serves as food for a wide variety of invertebrates such as shellfish and marine worms. The bay is home to a diverse range of wildlife, including eagles, ospreys, seals, otters, and occasionally bears. It also supports a rich fish population, including smelt, alewives, shad, sea-run brook trout, striped bass, and Atlantic salmon. The bay's productive food chain sustains over 200 bird species. Cobscook Bay's sheltered coves, mudflats, and eelgrass beds attract thousands of shorebirds each fall as they migrate south from their breeding grounds in the north. The bay's inner coves are a haven for wintering black ducks and boast the highest concentration of bald eagles in the state of Maine. Visitors can obtain a free birding list for the Cobscook Bay region at the park entrance. The geology of Cobscook Bay State Park is influenced by three main factors: the powerful tides of Cobscook Bay, the underlying bedrock composed of volcanic tuff-breccia formed around 420 million years ago during the Silurian Age, and the effects of glaciation from the Wisconsinan ice sheet that occurred approximately 12,000-18,000 years ago. The glacial activity deposited a mixture of mud, rocks, sand, silt, and clay called glacial till. These sedimentary layers cover the bedrock, usually reaching a thickness of no more than 10 feet. In areas where the bedrock is exposed, one can observe grooves on the rock surfaces, known as glacial striations, left by the movement of the ice sheet. In 1886, Nathaniel S. Shaler, one of the first geologists to explore the region, remarked that Cobscook Bay presents a collection of geological phenomena more captivating than any other part of the eastern seaboard of the United States. Cobscook Bay State Park is a part of Moosehorn National Wildlife Refuge, which was initially acquired in 1937 through funding from the federal Duck Stamp Program. Moosehorn, totaling 24,400 acres today, is one of the oldest wildlife refuges in the United States and was designated as a National Wildlife Refuge by President Franklin D. Roosevelt in 1937. President Roosevelt, who spent summers on the nearby Campobello Island in New Brunswick, played a crucial role in its establishment. In 1964, the Refuge granted the State of Maine a long-term lease at no cost for a "Recreation Area" that had been developed along Whiting Bay. After receiving approval from the Maine Legislature, the management of the area was transferred to the state, leading to the establishment of Cobscook Bay State Park. The creation of this park was made possible through funding from both the Land for Maine's Future program and the Land and Water Conservation Fund. When engaging in boating or exploring activities near the shore, it is essential to be cautious of the rapid and unpredictable changes in tides. Keep a close eye on children to ensure their safety. Although summer daytime temperatures usually average around 68°F (20°C), evenings and overcast days can feel chilly. Downeast Maine is renowned for its fog, so it's important to be ready for reduced visibility, especially when boating. During winter, anticipate daytime temperatures of approximately 18°F (-8°C), and exercise extra caution in snowy and icy conditions. In late spring and early summer, it is advisable to prepare for encounters with mosquitoes, black flies, and midges (also known as no-see-ums). While the area isn't heavily infested with deer ticks, it is still recommended to check yourself regularly to prevent Lyme disease. The campground at Cobscook Bay State Park operates from May 15 to October 15, providing an opportunity for visitors to enjoy camping during that period. However, the park's trails can be enjoyed throughout the year, regardless of the camping season. The peak time for shorebird migration in Cobscook Bay typically occurs in late August and early September. During the winter season, the park staff maintains trails for cross-country skiing and snowshoeing, as well as a sliding hill and a skating pond. The park offers two short trails suitable for walkers of all ages. The Nature Trail is a one-mile path that starts near the park entrance. It takes you through a forested area, follows alongside a brook, and then ascends to two scenic overlooks that provide views of Whiting Bay and Burnt Cove. The trail leading to the overlooks includes a short, steep, and rocky section, so it's important to exercise caution, especially in wet weather. Walkers can choose to return on a gravel road, making it a 2-mile round trip. The Shore Trail, also known as the Anthony's Beach Trail, is a 0.75-mile loop trail that begins near campsite 17. It runs parallel to the shore, passes by the boat launch, and then meanders through the woods before exiting between campsites 18 and 20. Many visitors also enjoy exploring the shoreline, but it's important to respect the privacy of waterfront campsites and be aware of the fast-moving tides. If you're not camping at the park but would like to access the trails, you can stop by the park entrance to obtain a map and pay the day-use fee. Fires are permitted only in provided grills or fireplaces. Please do not bring your own firewood. Purchase firewood locally or at the park to prevent the spread of invasive pests. Out-of-state firewood is prohibited. For more information, visit www.maine.gov/forestpests. Hunting is not allowed in this park. For hunting information and laws, visit www.maine.gov/ifw/. If there are no red tide warnings posted, campers may dig up to a peck of clams per person per day during the regulated season. Consult park staff for specific details. Cobscook Bay State Park is located within the Downeast-Acadia Region, which encompasses Hancock and Washington counties and represents the northeasternmost part of the United States. In close proximity to the park, there are several noteworthy destinations. Campobello Island in New Brunswick, Canada, accessible via the International Bridge from Lubec, is home to the historic Roosevelt Campobello International Park and East Quoddy Light. Quoddy Head State Park in Lubec features a picturesque lighthouse and scenic waterfront trails along the easternmost point of land in the United States. Roque Bluffs State Park, situated south of Machias, offers a lengthy pebble beach, hiking trails, picnic areas, a playground, and a freshwater pond. Cutler Coast Public Lands provide 10 miles of trails with 4.5 miles of coastline along the dramatic "Bold Coast." Moosehorn National Wildlife Refuge, located just one mile from Cobscook Bay State Park, offers a 6-mile wilderness loop trail.

NOTES:

PASSPORT STAMPS

CRESCENT BEACH STATE PARK

COUNTY: CUMBERLAND	ESTABLISHED: 1966	AREA (AC/HA): 242 / 97

DATE VISITED:　　　　**LODGING:**　　　　**WHO I WENT WITH:**

WEATHER: ☀☐ ☁☐ ☷☐ ❄☐ 🌧☐ 🌬☐　SPRING ☐ SUMMER ☐ FALL ☐ WINTER ☐

FEE(S):　　　　**RATING:** ☆ ☆ ☆ ☆ ☆　　　**WILL I RETURN?** YES / NO

Crescent Beach State Park, established in 1966, is a popular destination offering visitors the opportunity to enjoy swimming and sunbathing at one of Maine's most beautiful beaches. The park features sandy oceanfront beaches, saltwater coves, wooded areas, and rocky ledges, providing various recreational options for beachgoers, fishing enthusiasts, watersports lovers, and nature observers. At Crescent Beach State Park, visitors can find amenities such as picnic tables, grills, a children's playground, a snack bar, and a bathhouse equipped with cold-water showers. Adjacent to the park is Kettle Cove State Park, which offers stunning coastal views and a scenic walking trail that encircles the cove. The park is characterized by its mile-long, crescent-shaped beach, adorned with American beachgrass-studded sand dunes. The beach is perfect for leisurely strolls and sunbathing, and its relatively warm waters and gentle surf make swimming and boating enjoyable. Just a short distance away from the bustling summer sands, there are trails available for walking and observing nature. The park offers food services and a picnic area. During the off-season, when the park is closed to vehicles, walkers are welcome to experience the serenity of the beaches and trails. In winter, visitors can enjoy hiking or cross-country skiing on paths lined with snow-covered evergreen boughs, creating a picturesque winter landscape.

NOTES:

PASSPORT STAMPS

DAMARISCOTTA LAKE STATE PARK

COUNTY: LINCOLN	ESTABLISHED: 1970	AREA (AC/HA): 19 / 7.7

DATE VISITED:	LODGING:	WHO I WENT WITH:

WEATHER: ☀☐ ☁☐ ☔☐ ❄☐ 🌦☐ 🌬☐   SPRING ☐ SUMMER ☐ FALL ☐ WINTER ☐

FEE(S):	RATING: ☆ ☆ ☆ ☆ ☆	WILL I RETURN? YES / NO

Located in Jefferson, Damariscotta Lake State Park is a highly popular day-use park in midcoast Maine. It is conveniently situated near Augusta, the state's capital. The park offers a beautiful setting on Damariscotta Lake, where visitors can indulge in picnicking and swimming. The sandy beach provides a relaxing spot for beachgoers to unwind and enjoy the water. Damariscotta Lake State Park operates from 9:00 a.m. to sunset daily, starting from Memorial Day through Labor Day. A fee is required for entry into the park, and only cash or check payments are accepted. Credit cards are not applicable. During the off-season, visitors can still enjoy the park by parking outside the gate without obstructing it and walking in during the same hours. Please place the admission fee in the self-service collection canister. It's important to note that park facilities are closed during the off-season. Picnic tables and grills are available, making it an ideal location for summertime picnics. Additionally, the park offers a group picnic shelter equipped with electricity, running water, and a group grill. If you're interested in reserving the group shelter during the summer months, please contact the park staff. Due to limited parking availability on warm summer days, it is advisable to arrive early to secure a parking spot at the park. The park does not have a public boat launch available. However, visitors can access motorized boating through a state boat launch located halfway down the twelve-mile long lake.

NOTES:

PASSPORT STAMPS

FERRY BEACH STATE PARK

COUNTY: YORK	ESTABLISHED: -		AREA (AC/HA): 117 / 47
DATE VISITED:	LODGING:	WHO I WENT WITH:	
WEATHER: ☀☐ ☁☐ ☂☐ ❄☐ ☔☐ ☁☐		SPRING ☐ SUMMER ☐ FALL ☐ WINTER ☐	
FEE(S):	RATING: ☆ ☆ ☆ ☆ ☆	WILL I RETURN? YES / NO	

Ferry Beach State Park provides a picturesque setting with expansive views of miles of pristine white sand beaches stretching between the Saco River and Pine Point. This beach has been a beloved destination for generations, attracting sunbathers and swimmers. In addition to the beach, visitors can also explore the park's enchanting wooded paths and boardwalks. These trails meander through diverse ecosystems, including a captivating bog, a serene pond, and a unique tupelo swamp. The tupelo swamp is particularly noteworthy as it showcases a rare stand of tupelo (black gum) trees, which are uncommon at this latitude. Nature enthusiasts can further enhance their experience by visiting the park's nature center, which features informative exhibits and offers guided programs. To ensure you make the most of your visit, it is advisable to contact the park in advance to inquire about their scheduled hours and programs. In the days before highways became common north of Boston, beaches served as convenient and secure routes of transportation for travelers. At the nearby Saco River, a ferry crossing facilitated the transportation of beachgoers, giving rise to the name of Ferry Beach State Park. Between the years 1880 and 1923, there was a rail line that spanned 3.24 miles, connecting the Saco River at Camp Ellis to Old Orchard Beach. This rail line was operated by two small locomotive engines, each pulling two or three passenger cars with open sides. During the bustling summer tourist season, these trains ran daily from 6:00 a.m. to 10:30 p.m., making both set stops and stops upon request. One of the stops included Ferry Beach. This railway became known as the Dummy Railroad, possibly due to the small size of the engines and the open design of the passenger cars. It was also called the Dummy Railroad because the trains did not turn around. Instead, they would pull to Camp Ellis and then reverse (back up) to Old Orchard Beach. The fare for a roundtrip journey was 20 cents, and for an additional 25 cents, travelers could also enjoy a boat cruise to Wood Island from Camp Ellis. Ferry Beach is situated within the sandy landform that curves along the western side of Saco Bay. The sand found on the beach originated from glacial outwash during the last ice age, which came to an end approximately 10,000 years ago. As the Saco River carries sand downstream towards the ocean, it gets deposited at the river's mouth. From there, wave action picks up the sand and transports it further up the beach through a process known as littoral drift. Much of the sand settles on the beach and is then shaped into berms and dunes that run parallel to the shoreline. These dunes serve as natural barriers, protecting the coast from storms and high tides. Although the construction of dams along the river has somewhat reduced this process, it still continues to shape the beach. Tupelo Swamp likely formed shortly after the barrier beach was created, which blocked the flow of small brooks and streams towards the sea. While some water runoff from the land is redirected northward from Long Pond into Goosefare Brook, it tends to accumulate behind the dunes. The swamp experiences seasonal variations in water supply. In a typical year, water levels are highest in the spring and gradually decrease throughout the summer, only to be replenished by autumn rains. The true swamp conditions are primarily found in the upper parts of the drainages that feed the pond and along the slow-moving stream that flows north from the pond. In the early 1960s, portions of Long Pond were excavated and deepened to restore open water areas. Mounds of sand were piled up on the western shore of the pond, and trees have since grown on these mounds, creating the illusion of a natural landscape. The swamp serves as a unique habitat where various plant species have adapted to an environment that is sometimes more suitable for aquatic rather than terrestrial life. Trees like red maple, black tupelo, and willow thrive in the moist soil, providing a foundation for other plants in the swamp. When these trees fall during a storm and decay over time, they create organic mulch that nourishes new plant growth. The gaps left by their uprooted root systems form pools that support aquatic plants and insects. Additionally, a lone pine tree may sprout from a chance seed that landed on the soil-rich root mass from the nearby upland forest. Other plant species found in the swamp include cattail, blue flag iris, and ferns. The dense network of shrubs, such as highbush blueberry, maleberry, and winterberry (a type of holly), contributes to the impenetrable nature of the Tupelo Swamp. The growth of these shrubs, along with the presence of twining and thorny vines like greenbrier, often hinders forward movement within the swamp. The swamp floor and stumps in the Tupelo Swamp are covered by sphagnum moss, a remarkable plant that forms a spongy layer. This moss has the ability to store a significant amount of water, up to twenty times its weight, and plays a crucial role in providing moisture to other plants during periods of dryness. Sphagnum moss has the potential to transform into peat, contributing to the formation of rich peat deposits. The swamp is teeming with insect life, creating a thriving ecosystem that attracts a variety of birds, small mammals, and amphibians. The presence of frogs is particularly noticeable during the early spring chorus when their calls fill the air. While larger animals are uncommon in the area due to human activities, occasional sightings of deer in the park's vicinity do occur. The boundary between the swamp and the upland forest is typically clear and distinguishable. At the points where small streams from drainage areas intersect with the swamp, wet conditions may extend further into the higher areas. Similarly, sections of the upland forest may extend into the swamp, with only a slight increase in soil depth of a foot or two. The upland forest primarily consists of a mix of white pine, northern red oak, and hemlock trees, along with beech, birch, and maple. During the 1950s, the area underwent logging, which resulted in the removal of mature pine trees. However, since then, the forest has regenerated naturally, and there is little evidence of the previous logging activities, as the second-growth forest has successfully established itself. This park is for day-use only, and camping is not permitted. Vehicles must stay on designated roads and park only in designated parking spaces. Visitors should stay on designated trails or boardwalks to protect the land. Fires are only permitted in designated grills. Visitors should use charcoal as the fuel for your fire. Practice a carry-in, carry-out approach for picnicking. Dogs are not allowed on the ocean beach from April 1 to September 30. In other areas, pets must be leashed, attended, and under control at all times. The park offers numerous loop options and trail combinations to explore the park's diverse habitats. The trails are open to the public year-round, but in late fall, winter and early spring signs are temporarily removed for storage and maintenance. The Tupelo Trail, an easy 0.36-mile path, takes you across a boardwalk that overlooks a beautiful pocket swamp adorned with ferns, mosses, and the remarkable tupelo trees that give this trail its name. Along the way, you'll encounter a picnic table where you can pause and enjoy the scenic view of Long Pond. As you continue, the trail leads you into the heart of the tupelo swamp via a second boardwalk, allowing you to get up close to the tupelo trees and their distinctively thick, blocky bark resembling alligator hide. The trail concludes at the intersection with the Red Oak Trail. To access the Tupelo Trail, start at the northeast corner parking lot and remember to keep to the right at all trail crossings to stay on this specific route. For a longer and more diverse 1-mile easy loop that showcases several unique features of the park, you can combine the Tupelo Trail with the Red Oak and White Oak Trails. Alternatively, shorter loops can be created by combining the Tupelo Trail with either the Greenbriar or Witch Hazel Trails. The Red Oak Trail, an easy 0.30-mile path, offers a chance to spot the red oaks that lend their name to this trail, recognizable by their pointed leaf tips. Keep an eye on the forest floor, particularly in late summer, as you may come across the yellow spindle coral mushrooms. The trail culminates at the north end of Long Pond, where a bench awaits, providing a perfect vantage point to admire the entire length of the pond. To access the Red Oak Trail, you can follow the park entry road and choose to explore it as an out-and-back route. Alternatively, you can combine it with the White Oak and Tupelo Trails to form a 1-mile loop, commencing from the parking lot. The White Oak Trail, an easy 0.30-mile path, offers a refreshing and shaded escape after a day spent on the beach. This trail winds its way through a hemlock forest and concludes at the Red Oak Trail. To access the White Oak Trail, start at the northeast corner parking lot and remember to keep left at all trail crossings to stay on this trail. Alternatively, you can connect to it from the picnic area trail located at the northwest corner of the parking lot. The Witch Hazel Trail, an easy 0.057-mile (or 300 feet) trail, connects the Tupelo Trail to the White Oak Trail, forming a half-mile loop that starts and finishes at the parking lot. The Greenbriar Trail, an easy 0.10-mile path, links the Tupelo Trail to the White Oak Trail, creating a 0.4-mile loop with both the start and finish at the parking lot.

NOTES:

PASSPORT STAMPS

FORT POINT STATE PARK

COUNTY: WALDO		ESTABLISHED: 1974		AREA (AC/HA): 120 / 48

DATE VISITED:	LODGING:		WHO I WENT WITH:	

WEATHER: ☀☐ ☁☐ ☔☐ ❄☐ ⛈☐ ☁☐		SPRING ☐ SUMMER ☐ FALL ☐ WINTER ☐	

FEE(S):	RATING: ☆ ☆ ☆ ☆ ☆	WILL I RETURN? YES / NO

One of the main attractions of Fort Point State Park is its scenic features, such as picnic tables with a view of the waterfront, a pier and floats for fishing and boating, and access to a beautiful biking trip. The park is located in Stockton Springs, around three miles away from U.S. Route 1. Its name originates from the point where Gov. Thomas Pownall established Fort Pownall in 1759. Situated on a long peninsula, the park offers breathtaking views of the Penobscot River and Penobscot Bay. It covers an area of 120 acres and includes over a mile of rocky shore, a tidal sandbar, and diverse habitats that support various plant and animal species. The park, which was opened in 1974, also encompasses Fort Point State Historic Site and the Fort Point Light Station. From around 500 to 1,000 B.C., the Penobscot River valley was inhabited by Native Americans who were the ancestors of the Etchemins and the present-day Penobscot tribe. These indigenous people relied on climate changes, geographical factors, and the seasonal abundance of food for their way of life. Some of these groups may have focused on utilizing coastal resources, residing in different locations either permanently or repeatedly throughout the year. Meanwhile, others engaged in seasonal migration, moving between inland areas and the coastline to meet their needs. For over a century, France and England had been locked in a conflict over the ownership of North American territories. In 1758, Governor Thomas Pownall of Massachusetts emphasized the crucial significance of establishing a fort at the Penobscot River for the English. According to Pownall, such a fort would grant the English control over a splendid land and the finest bay in North America. Additionally, it would serve as a strategic measure to keep the French and their Native American allies at a distance from the coast. In May 1759, Governor Pownall led a group of 400 men to construct Fort Pownall, a fortification that showcased an exceptional design for its time and location. The fort featured a spacious central blockhouse with four bastions, surrounded by a palisade, ditch, and a large earthen bank, all arranged in the shape of a four-pointed star. Shortly after the completion of Fort Pownall, the English successfully captured Quebec, thereby putting an end to France's foothold in North America. Although Fort Pownall did not fulfill its intended military objectives, its presence played a role in facilitating later English settlement in the Penobscot region. Furthermore, the fort served as a hub for trade activities, contributing to the development of commerce in the area. Tensions reached a boiling point in this area just before the outbreak of the American Revolution. With the consent of the Loyalist leader overseeing Fort Pownall, British sailors landed one night in March 1775 and clandestinely took away the fort's cannons to prevent them from falling into the hands of the rebels. In response, American revolutionaries set fire to the blockhouse and filled in the surrounding moat to obstruct any potential British occupation of the fort. Established in 1836 to assist the increasing number of ships navigating the Penobscot River between Bangor and Castine, the Fort Point Light Station was constructed as Maine's first river light. In 1857, the original granite structures were replaced with the current tower and keeper's house. The light station features a fixed white light, powered by a fourth-order Fresnel lens and a 250-watt halogen bulb, positioned 88 feet above sea level, and visible for over 10 miles. The fog signal, a 1,200-pound cast iron bell suspended on a pyramidal tower built in 1890, remains visible to this day. For more than 120 years, civilian keepers employed by the U.S. Lighthouse Establishment were responsible for maintaining this light station until the Coast Guard assumed operational duties in 1957. Presently, the light station is operated by Maine's Bureau of Parks and Lands as a historic site, equipped with automated lighting and a fog signal. In 1872, the construction of the Fort Point Hotel marked the beginning of Fort Point's attraction for tourists. This hotel had the capacity to accommodate around 200 guests, primarily consisting of wealthy individuals from Boston and New York City who would arrive by steamboat. The Fort Point Hotel aimed to rival the popularity of Bar Harbor and boasted luxurious amenities such as running water, gas lights, stables, a bowling alley, and two dance pavilions. It was designed to cater to an upscale clientele. Despite its ambitions, the Fort Point Hotel faced a series of challenges. It changed ownership four times and underwent several name changes. Unfortunately, just before its scheduled seasonal opening, the hotel was tragically destroyed by fire in May 1898. This setback ultimately led to the failure of the hotel and dashed hopes of establishing Fort Point as a prominent tourist destination. Within the park, visitors can explore the remains of Fort Pownall, where they can find interpretive panels and a stone marker indicating the original burial site of Gen. Samuel Waldo, after whom Waldo County and Waldoboro are named. Just a short walk from the parking lot, visitors can enjoy riverside picnic areas and prepare themselves for activities like hiking, sightseeing, biking, fishing, or paddling. Well-maintained trails guide hikers through fields and forests, leading to rocky shores and historical sites. Informational signs provide insights into Fort Point's history as a military, maritime, and tourist hub. Cyclists can follow the roads from the parking lot to reach the lighthouse or embark on a seven-mile loop around Cape Jellison. In winter, visitors can engage in cross-country skiing on the park's hiking trails and closed roads. Nature enthusiasts and wildlife watchers are treated to a diverse array of animal sightings at Fort Point State Park. On land, one can spot deer, foxes, snowshoe hares, porcupines, owls, and occasionally even moose. Along the shoreline, there is an opportunity to observe wading birds, sea ducks, shorebirds, and majestic loons. For a closer encounter with marine life, the park's pier extends 200 feet into the river, providing an excellent vantage point. Visitors can keep an eye out for seals or porpoises swimming in the water, while ospreys and bald eagles soar overhead. The pier and tidal sandbar are particularly popular among anglers, who can try their luck catching salmon, mackerel, and striped bass. With the convenience of seasonal floats, the pier also serves as a launching point for kayaks and canoes, allowing visitors to embark on peaceful paddling excursions. It is also a convenient docking spot for those arriving by powerboat, sailboat, or even a traditional windjammer. Fort Point State Park is open for visitors daily from 9:00 a.m. until sunset between May 15 and October 15, unless there are specific notices posted at the entrance. During the off season, visitors can still enjoy the park by parking their vehicles outside the gate and walking in during the same hours. However, it's important to note that the park's facilities are closed during the off season. In the surrounding area, there are numerous attractions and destinations worth exploring. These include various state parks and historic sites, such as Fort Knox State Historic Site, Holbrook Island Sanctuary, Camden Hills State Park, Moose Point State Park, and Swan Lake State Park. Within a convenient hour's drive from Fort Point, visitors will discover a wide range of amenities and activities. There are accommodations available, as well as restaurants offering diverse dining options. Art enthusiasts can explore art galleries showcasing local talent, and there is also a museum and a theater for cultural experiences. For those interested in local produce and goods, a farmer's market is available. Bicycle and kayak rentals offer opportunities for outdoor adventures, while craft, antique, and gift shops cater to those seeking unique treasures.

NOTES:

PASSPORT STAMPS

GRAFTON NOTCH STATE PARK

COUNTY: OXFORD		ESTABLISHED: 1963		AREA (AC/HA): 3,129 / 1,266
DATE VISITED:	LODGING:		WHO I WENT WITH:	
WEATHER: ☀☐ ☁☐ ☔☐ ❄☐ ⛆☐ ☁☐			SPRING ☐ SUMMER ☐ FALL ☐ WINTER ☐	
FEE(S):	RATING: ☆ ☆ ☆ ☆ ☆		WILL I RETURN? YES / NO	

Grafton Notch State Park and the Mahoosuc Public Lands are highly sought-after destinations for outdoor recreation, nestled amidst the breathtaking mountains of the Mahoosuc Range in Maine. These lands offer rugged and challenging terrain, making them ideal for backcountry hikers. In fact, they encompass 12 of the most demanding miles along the entire Appalachian Trail. Hikers who brave the steep trails to reach the summits are rewarded with awe-inspiring views, especially from the top of Old Speck Mountain, which stands at 4,180 feet. For those seeking less strenuous adventures, there are shorter walks that lead to impressive waterfalls and stunning gorges. The renowned Grafton Notch Scenic Byway cuts through the park, offering several pull-offs where visitors can admire interesting natural features. Grafton Notch State Park, which is part of the Maine Birding Trail, provides birdwatchers with opportunities to observe peregrine falcons, a diverse array of songbirds, and, at higher elevations, species typically found in northern forests. Even at lower elevations near Route 26, it is common to spot large mammals. Hunters frequent the area in search of deer, bear, and grouse, while fishermen try their luck catching brook trout in the numerous streams. During winter, snowshoers, cross-country skiers, and snowmobilers relish the chance to explore these lands. The popular snowmobile route ITS 82 traverses this region, running from Andover to New Hampshire's Trail 18. Within the Mahoosuc Public Lands, there is a designated 9,993-acre Ecological Reserve, recognized by the state for preserving sensitive ecosystems in their natural state and facilitating long-term monitoring of ecological changes. The reserve encompasses a sub-alpine tarn called Speck Pond and harbors several rare plant and animal species. The Maine Bureau of Parks and Lands oversees the management of certain sections of the Mahoosuc Public Land Unit, including timber production, which contributes to the maintenance costs of the public lands. These timber management practices are certified as sustainable, ensuring the preservation of the lands while supporting their upkeep. Grafton Notch State Park and the Mahoosuc Public Lands offer a captivating journey through Maine's geological past and serve as a living testament to the transformative power of water in shaping the landscape. The presence of metamorphic bedrock, formed around 420 million years ago, is evident in certain areas, such as the summit of Old Speck Mountain. Grafton Notch showcases a classic example of a U-shaped valley, carved by the action of glaciers during the last ice age. Remnants of this glacial activity can still be seen on higher mountain ledges, marked by striations or grooves left by the moving ice. Additionally, there are numerous deposits of sand and gravel outwash, remnants of the glacial meltwater. Approximately 12,000 years ago, the glaciers receded from this region. However, the process of erosion continues to this day, as water gradually moves stones, creating potholes and exploiting weak points in the underlying rock formations. This ongoing erosion shapes and modifies the landscape, highlighting the dynamic nature of geological processes. Visitors to Grafton Notch State Park and the Mahoosuc Public Lands have the opportunity to witness the remarkable results of millions of years of geological history and the continuous impact of water on the land, providing a unique perspective on the ever-changing nature of our planet. The waterfalls and gorges within the area exhibit their most breathtaking beauty during late spring, when the melting snow contributes to increased river volume. It is crucial to exercise caution around the cold and swiftly flowing waters during this period. Hikers find great delight in exploring the region during the warmer months, while many visitors flock to witness the spectacular display of autumn foliage. In winter, resilient cross-country skiers and snowshoers venture onto the ungroomed trails, while snowmobilers revel in the trails at lower elevations. There are many trails available to visitors. Route 26 (Appalachian Trail) Trailhead: The designated parking area located along Route 26 offers amenities such as a pit toilet, a trail register, and brochures. It serves as a starting point for day hiking and overnight backpacking adventures. From this trailhead, hikers can access both the Appalachian Trail (AT) and the Grafton Loop Trail. The Grafton Loop Trail branches off the AT in both the north and south directions from the Route 26 trailhead, providing additional backpacking opportunities. Popular day hikes in the area include the Table Rock Trail and the Appalachian Trail leading to the summit of Old Speck. The Grafton Loop Trail is a challenging backcountry trail that spans 38 miles and typically takes three or more days to complete. It offers a high-elevation experience and showcases the beauty of the region. Along the trail, there are seven primitive campsites available for overnight stays. The trail connects a series of nine scenic peaks, including notable landmarks like Old Speck, Sunday River Whitecap, Puzzle Mountain, and East and West Baldpate. While the northern sections of the Grafton Loop Trail follow the Appalachian Trail (AT), the majority of the trail is relatively new and owes its existence to the hard work of numerous volunteers, partners, and the generosity of private landowners. It's important to note that certain sections of the trail pass through private land. Additionally, it's worth mentioning that the Grafton Loop Trail intersects with Route 26 at another location further south, near Eddy Rd. in North Newry. The designated parking area for this intersection is located on the eastern side of Route 26, near the trailhead for Puzzle Mountain. If you wish to access the southwestern portion of the Grafton Loop Trail, you can walk approximately 0.75 miles south on Route 26 from the parking area to reach the trailhead. On the west side of Route 26, there are two notable trails: the Old Speck Trail and the Eyebrow Loop Trail. The Old Speck Trail is a challenging 7.6-mile hike that takes approximately 7 hours to complete. It offers breathtaking views from an open observation tower at the summit. To begin the trail, follow the white-blazed Appalachian Trail south along Cascade Brook. Along the way, you'll cross several streams before ascending the north shoulder of the mountain. As you ascend, you'll be treated to frequent views of the Notch. The summit and observation tower can be reached by taking a 0.3-mile spur trail, which is approximately 3.5 miles from the trailhead. From the summit, the Grafton Loop Trail continues, descending southeastward. The Eyebrow Loop Trail is another challenging option, covering 2.2 miles round trip and taking about 2-3 hours to complete. This trail leads to an "eyebrow" shelf/overlook on Old Speck Mountain, situated at an elevation of 2,900 feet. To access the Eyebrow Loop Trail, follow the white-blazed Appalachian Trail south for 0.1 miles from the starting point. You'll then reach the beginning of the orange-blazed Eyebrow Trail. As you hike, you'll pass through magnificent hardwoods, gradually ascending until you reach a steeper section with precipices. In some parts of the ascent, there are ladders or steel rungs to assist in climbing. The descent follows the Appalachian Trail, which is steep but doesn't require climbing aids. If you prefer to avoid the rungs and ladders, you can opt to hike up and back along the Appalachian Trail for a round trip of 2.6 miles. Please note that the Eyebrow Loop Trail may not be suitable for small children, especially in wet conditions. On the east side of Route 26, there are several trails worth exploring: the Table Rock Loop Trail, the Baldpate Mountain Trail, and the Appalachian Trail. The Table Rock Loop Trail is a moderate hike covering 2.4 miles round trip and taking approximately 2 hours to complete. The trail begins near Route 26. Start by following the white-blazed Appalachian Trail north for 0.1 miles. At this point, you have two options: you can choose the steep and boulder-strewn orange-blazed Table Rock Trail (not suitable for pets or young children), or you can continue on the moderately steep Appalachian Trail to the next trail junction. After approximately one mile, the blue-blazed Table Rock Trail begins, offering an easier hike for less experienced hikers. Table Rock, which is 900 feet above your starting point, offers fantastic views of Old Speck, the Eyebrow, and Grafton Notch. Be cautious at the summit as there is a steep drop-off where the ledge ends, and there is no fencing. The Baldpate Mountain Trail is a challenging option, offering a round trip of 5.8 miles to West Peak or 7.6 miles to East Peak. It is recommended to allocate 7 hours for this hike. To access the trail, follow the white-blazed Appalachian Trail north from Route 26. As you enter the Mahoosuc Public Lands, the trail steadily ascends across the north slope, leading to the open summit of West Baldpate, which stands at an elevation of 3,680 feet. Continuing north, the trail descends only 240 feet in altitude before climbing for nearly a mile to East Peak, reaching an elevation of 3,812 feet. East Peak offers outstanding views in all directions. The Appalachian Trail in this area spans over 20 miles and is considered challenging. It is characterized by steep and boulder-strewn sections as it follows ridgelines through the Mahoosuc Range, including Grafton Notch State Park and the Mahoosuc Public Lands. One of the most difficult stretches is between Full Goose Lean-to and Speck Pond Lean-to. Hikers attempting this stretch should be well-conditioned and properly equipped. Trailheads along Success Pond Road provide access to various trails leading into Grafton Notch State Park and the Mahoosuc Public Lands. There are three trailheads in total, accessible via unmarked logging roads. The Speck Pond Trail is a challenging 3.2-mile one-way hike, taking approximately 3 hours to complete. It follows a small stream and then ascends eastward, crossing Mahoosuc Arm before reaching Speck Pond and joining the

Appalachian Trail. The Mahoosuc Notch Trail is a very challenging 2.3-mile one-way hike, requiring about 1.5 hours. It joins the Appalachian Trail just south of Mahoosuc Notch. Many hikers consider this section to be the most demanding part of the entire Appalachian Trail. Expect to navigate over, around, between, and underneath massive rock slabs. The Goose Eye Trail is a moderately challenging option, covering 3.1 miles one way and taking approximately 3 hours. It shares a trailhead with the Carlo Col Trail and provides access to Goose Eye Mountain and the Appalachian Trail. The Carlo Col Trail is an easier hike, spanning 2.6 miles one way and taking around 2 hours. It ascends gently to Carlo Col, which is a gap between two mountain peaks, and joins the Appalachian Trail. Please note that accessing these trailheads requires navigating unmarked logging roads. The Bull Branch Road Trailhead offers access to the Wright Trail, which is a challenging 8.5-mile round trip hike. It takes approximately 8 hours to complete and leads hikers through mature forests to the bald east peak of Goose Eye Mountain. Along the trail, expect to encounter rugged terrain and a rigorous hiking experience. The trail follows Goose Eye Brook initially and then ascends to join the Appalachian Trail, eventually reaching the open summit area of Goose Eye Mountain. From the summit, hikers are rewarded with stunning panoramic views in all directions. The East B Hill Road Trailheads provide access to the Cataracts Trail, which is an easy 0.4-mile hike taking approximately 0.5 hours to complete. The trail leads hikers to a beautiful gorge where Frye Brook cascades over several waterfalls, situated between Baldpate and Surplus mountains. Adjacent to the falls, there is a day-use area that offers a pleasant spot for a lunch break. It's important to note that the Cataracts Trail does not serve as an official and maintained access point to the Appalachian Trail (AT) or Baldpate Mountain. However, the AT does intersect with East B Hill Road, located approximately 2.5 miles north of the Cataracts trailhead. The western half of the property features the ITS 82 snowmobile trail, providing a route for snowmobile riders. Additionally, ATV riders have the option to utilize a section of shared-use road located off the Sunday River Road in the Riley Township portion of the Mahoosuc Unit. Here are some important guidelines to follow when visiting the region: Exercise caution while driving on area roads, especially during low light conditions, as the region is home to abundant large animals. Drive slowly and remain alert. Additionally, ensure that your tents and their contents are free of food and food odors to avoid attracting wildlife. Do not solely rely on your cell phone in case of emergencies, as the coverage in the area may be unreliable or non-existent. Be prepared with alternative communication methods or emergency devices. Potable water is not available at the Park, so it is necessary to bring your own. If you need to access water from brooks or ponds within the park, make sure to purify it before consumption. During winter, parking options for users include the lot off Route 26 or the twin bridges on the Sunday River Road. Expect weather conditions to change rapidly, especially at higher elevations. The mountains experience early snowfall and prolonged snow cover. Be prepared for these conditions and plan accordingly. The park is characterized by rock outcroppings and rugged terrain, which can add challenges to hikes. Exercise extra caution during wet conditions. Wear appropriate footwear and clothing, and closely supervise children. It's important to know your limits and be willing to turn back if needed. It's possible that there are private properties within and adjacent to the public lands. Respect any landowner restrictions and be mindful that the public use of these areas is a privilege, not an inherent right. Keep pets on a leash and under control at all times while in the park. Carry out all trash and dispose of it properly. Leave no trace behind. The use of intoxicating beverages is prohibited in the park. Respect the natural and historical features of the park. Do not pick or remove anything from the environment. Leave it for others to enjoy. Observe wildlife from a distance and refrain from feeding or disturbing animals or birds. It's important to maintain a safe distance and not disrupt their natural behavior. Camping is not allowed at Grafton Notch State Park. However, low-impact camping is permitted only on the Public Lands. Fires are only allowed at designated sites, and fires are not permitted at campsites located on private lands along the Grafton Loop Trail. When grills are provided, only use them for charcoal fires. Hunting is not permitted at Grafton Notch State Park between June 1 and Labor Day. However, hunting on the Public Lands follows the state's hunting seasons. Refer to the Maine Department of Inland Fisheries and Wildlife website (www.maine.gov/ifw) for information on Maine's fishing and hunting laws, as well as license requirements. The discharge of any weapon is strictly prohibited within 300 feet of any picnic area, camping area, parking area, posted trail, or other developed area. Loaded firearms are not allowed at campsites or on hiking trails. Noteworthy Attractions: Screw Auger Falls: A pathway accessible from Route 26 leads to this captivating waterfall, which measures 23 feet in height. It is situated within a narrow gorge along the Bear River. While many visitors enjoy wading in the shallow pools, it is important to closely supervise children and avoid venturing near the edge of the falls. Mother Walker Falls: This impressive V-shaped gorge, named after a local resident, stretches over 40 feet deep and spans 980 feet in length. It is a short walk from Route 26. Please exercise caution and closely supervise children while exploring this area. Moose Cave: Nestled within a 45-foot-deep canyon of bedrock, this 200-foot-long gorge showcases the mesmerizing sight of water winding its way around boulders before temporarily vanishing into a cave beneath a massive granite slab. The loop trail to Moose Cave, accessible from Route 26, spans a quarter-mile and features some narrow sections and steep slopes. Spruce Meadow Picnic Area: Located in the northern part of the park, this picturesque spot provides a serene setting with tables equipped with grills. Visitors can enjoy their meals while overlooking a marsh teeming with wildlife and the scenic Old Speck Mountain. The Grafton-Mahoosuc lands are located within Maine's Lakes and Region, encompassing Franklin and Oxford Counties, in close proximity to the following destinations: Mt. Blue State Park: This park attracts visitors with its camping facilities, opportunities for swimming in Webb Lake, hiking trails, mountain biking routes, and the chance to ride ATVs and horses. Richardson Lakes Public Lands: Offering a serene and secluded backcountry experience, these lands feature scenic paddling routes and primitive campsites (managed by South Arm Campground) across 22,000 preserved acres in the renowned Rangeley Lakes region. Lake Umbagog National Wildlife Refuge:

Situated along the New Hampshire border, this refuge spans a vast 7,850-acre water body. It provides backcountry campsites and is a haven for spectacular wildlife viewing experiences. Other Points of Interest: Frenchman's Hole: This attraction lures people during hot weather as they indulge in swimming and picnicking by the crystal-clear waters and captivating rock formations of Bull Branch Stream. Step Falls Preserve: Owned and managed by the Maine Chapter of The Nature Conservancy, this preserve offers a delightful one-hour roundtrip walk alongside a series of cascading pools on Wight Brook, featuring a total drop of 250 feet. The preserve is located half a mile southeast of Grafton Notch State Park along Route 26. State Route 26: Designated as a scenic byway by the state, this route stretches from Newry to the New Hampshire border. It captivates travelers with its awe-inspiring mountains, breathtaking gorges, and enchanting waterfalls along the Bear River valley.

NOTES:

PASSPORT STAMPS

HOLBROOK ISLAND SANCTUARY STATE PARK

COUNTY: HANCOCK	ESTABLISHED: 1971	AREA (AC/HA): 115 / 46

DATE VISITED:	LODGING:	WHO I WENT WITH:

WEATHER: ☀☐ ☁☐ ☔☐ ❄☐ ⛈☐ 🌫☐ SPRING ☐ SUMMER ☐ FALL ☐ WINTER ☐

FEE(S):	RATING: ☆ ☆ ☆ ☆ ☆	WILL I RETURN? YES / NO

Holbrook Island is located in eastern Penobscot Bay, approximately 0.4 miles away from the mainland portion of Holbrook Island Sanctuary. The island is surrounded by rocky ledges, sandy beaches, and mud flats. It spans about a mile in length and encompasses approximately 115 acres of wooded areas and fields. Despite its forested appearance, the island has a rich human history. According to Anita Harris, the island's previous private owner, Holbrook Island was settled shortly after the Revolutionary War by Capt. Jesse Holbrook from Truro, Massachusetts. The island played a significant role in providing tall pines for the construction of sailing ships in the nearby town of Castine. It is said that one of the subsequent owners of the island kept his mistress there, and their daughter spent most of her life tending to sheep on the island. In 1891, Edward Kelleran Harris purchased the island from the daughter for $500. He cleared more fields for farming and constructed a summer home for his family. Anita Harris, the daughter of Edward Harris, was the last surviving member of the family and resided on the island until her passing in 1985. Anita Harris, a passionate nature lover with a special affinity for animals, bequeathed her island to the State of Maine with a stipulation that it be preserved and maintained as a wildlife and natural area. Honoring her wishes, the majority of the structures on the island have been removed, allowing it to revert to its natural state. In order to ensure the island's protection, Miss Harris' will prohibits the establishment of picnic facilities, the use of motorized vehicles, commercial activities, road construction, hunting, fishing, and trapping. Within these guidelines, the Maine Bureau of Parks and Lands manages the island, facilitating appropriate and low-impact utilization of the area. The primary focus is on preserving the island's natural environment and wildlife while allowing visitors to enjoy the island's offerings in a sustainable manner. Hikers and nature lovers can explore the sanctuary's trails and appreciate the beauty of the surroundings. In the winter, the sanctuary also offers opportunities for cross-country skiing. For those looking to have a picnic, there are picnic tables available for use. Additionally, there is an area designated for launching canoes and kayaks, allowing visitors to further explore the scenic waterways. The sanctuary is home to a wide array of plant and animal life, thanks to its varied landscapes. From the sandy beaches, mud flats, and rocky coastline to the rugged hills that were once volcanoes, there is a wealth of natural diversity to discover. The sanctuary's forests feature spruce-fir, pine, and mixed hardwoods, creating a habitat that supports an abundance of vibrant wildflowers throughout the seasons, from early spring to late fall. As visitors traverse the forests, fields, marshes, and ponds, they may encounter various signs of wildlife. Deer, foxes, muskrats, beavers, otters, porcupines, bobcats, and coyotes are among the animals that can be observed in their natural habitat within the sanctuary. It is a place where nature thrives, providing a serene and immersive experience for all who visit. Visitors can explore the beauty of the park using the following trails. Mud Cove Trail, spanning a distance of 0.25 miles, offers an easy walk leading to Mud Cove. Along the shoreline, the Lookout Point Trail extends for 0.24 miles, providing a straightforward path to Lookout Point. Through the forest, the Northwest Cove Trail stretches for 0.34 miles, offering excellent opportunities for bird watching and wildlife sightings. For a journey to Marsh Point Trail, covering a distance of 0.25 miles, visitors can proceed to the Southeast Cove Trail and Arrowhead Beach Trail. This trail provides an easy walk and serves as a prime location for bird watching and observing wildlife. The Southeast Cove Trail spans 0.05 miles and leads to a lovely small beach, offering a lookout point to the waterway between Nautilus and Holbrook Island. Lastly, the Arrowhead Beach Trail measures 0.02 miles and leads to an area with shale and flint, where it is said that Native Americans discovered materials for crafting their arrowheads. Please adhere to the following rules and regulations while visiting the park: The park is open from 9:00 am until sunset. Camping is strictly prohibited within the park and on the Island. Dogs must be kept on a leash at all times and are not allowed on the beaches. Open fires are not allowed on the Island or the beaches. However, charcoal cookers and Coleman stoves are permitted on the beaches. A donation can is available by the floats. The proceeds from donations contribute to the maintenance and upkeep of the Park and Island. There is one visitor mooring near the docks on the Island. Two visitor moorings are located in Tom Cod Cove on the mainland.

NOTES:

PASSPORT STAMPS

LAKE ST. GEORGE STATE PARK

COUNTY: WALDO	ESTABLISHED: -	AREA (AC/HA): 358 / 144
DATE VISITED:	LODGING:	WHO I WENT WITH:

WEATHER: ☼☐ ☁☐ ☁☐ ❄☐ ☂☐ ☁☐	SPRING ☐ SUMMER ☐ FALL ☐ WINTER ☐

FEE(S):	RATING: ☆ ☆ ☆ ☆ ☆	WILL I RETURN? YES / NO

Lake St. George State Park is situated on the northwest shore of the picturesque Lake St. George, approximately 16 miles west of Belfast and 25 miles east of Augusta. State Route 3 runs parallel to the lake, which was originally part of a farmstead. The main highlight of the park is the stunning Lake St. George itself. Some of the campsites are situated right by the lakeshore, allowing campers to enjoy a morning cup of coffee while observing the sunrise over the clear water. Frequent visitors to the park are loons, whose distinctive calls can often be heard at night. The lake spans 1,017 acres and contains several undeveloped islands scattered across its main basin. Fishing for landlocked salmon, bass, and brook trout is a popular sport in the area. In winter, ice fishing is a popular activity at the park. Youth can participate and hone their skills at the annual Youth Ice Fishing Derby. The day-use area, which is a short walk from the campground, provides picnic tables and grills by the lakeside, as well as swings, a horseshoe pit, basketball court, and a sandpit for young children. These amenities are conveniently located near the swim beach. Additionally, there is a group picnic shelter that overlooks the beach and day-use area. For those interested in exploring the park's undeveloped shoreline, a variety of watercraft such as canoes, paddleboats, rowboats, paddleboards, and kayaks are available for rent on-site. Hikers will delight in the fact that three to five miles of hiking trails are easily accessible from the campground, providing ample opportunities for exploration and outdoor adventures. Walking within the park is easy south of Route 3. However, north of Route 3, hikers can embark on the steep and forested 0.5-mile River Trail, which leads to the Frye Mt-Liberty Trail. The Frye Mt-Liberty Trail, maintained by local snowmobile clubs, offers a longer and more challenging hiking experience. The park operates from 9:00 a.m. until sunset on a daily basis, unless there are specific notices posted at the entrance gate. Upon entry, visitors are required to pay a fee, which can be done at the entry booth with the assistance of park staff or through the self-service station. Those interested in accessing all State Parks & Historic Sites can obtain an Annual Park Pass either at the entry booth or online at www.mainestateparkpass.com. The park offers 40 spacious campsites, both waterfront and surrounded by trees, each equipped with fireplaces and picnic tables. Campers have access to flush toilets, hot showers, water spigots, and a trailer dumping station. Camping reservations can be made online at www.campwithme.com. Quiet hours are enforced from 10:00 p.m. to 7:00 a.m. at the campsites. Generators can be used between 8:00 a.m. and 8:00 p.m. as long as the noise does not disturb other visitors. Visitors can enjoy a sandy beach and a designated swimming area. Watercraft rentals are available for those interested. The park has a trailer boat launch adjacent to its premises. An online sortable listing of boat launches can be found at www.maine.gov/dacf/boatlaunches. A group picnic shelter can be reserved by contacting the park directly. Fires are permitted only in designated park fireplaces and grills. Pets must be kept on a leash, attended to, and under control at all times. All trash must be carried out by campers. There is a dumping station available for their use. Fishing is allowed, but a valid fishing license and familiarity with the State's open water fishing regulations are required. Anglers are encouraged to use lead-free sinkers and jigs to prevent metal poisoning in loons, eagles, and other wildlife. Information can be found at www.maine.gov/ifw/. Weapons should not be discharged within 300 feet of any picnic or parking area, marked trail, or other developed areas. Details about hunting licenses and seasons can be found at www.maine.gov/ifw/.

NOTES:

PASSPORT STAMPS

LAMOINE STATE PARK

COUNTY: HANCOCK	ESTABLISHED: 1950S	AREA (AC/HA): 55 / 22

DATE VISITED:	LODGING:	WHO I WENT WITH:

WEATHER: ☀☐ ☁☐ ☷☐ ❄☐ 🌧☐ 🌊☐   SPRING ☐ SUMMER ☐ FALL ☐ WINTER ☐

FEE(S):	RATING: ☆ ☆ ☆ ☆ ☆	WILL I RETURN? YES / NO

Located in the heart of Downeast Maine, Lamoine State Park is situated along the oceanfront in one of the most desirable vacation regions in the state. Its central location provides a peaceful alternative for visitors seeking easy access to popular destinations such as Bar Harbor, Acadia National Park, enchanting rockbound islands, and local lighthouses. The park offers a range of activities, including camping, boating, kayaking, fishing, hunting, and simple relaxation, all set in a stunning and scenic environment. Notable features of the park include picturesque views of Frenchman's Bay and amenities such as well-maintained campground facilities and a convenient boat launching ramp. During the early 1900s, the area along the waterfront where the park is currently located served as a U.S. Navy coaling station. This facility was established in 1902 but became obsolete by 1912 due to advancements in technology that rendered coal-burning warships and their refueling stations no longer necessary. The state of Maine acquired ownership of the property in 1949 and subsequently transformed it into a state park during the 1950s. From May 15 to October 15, Lamoine State Park is open daily from 9:00 a.m. until sunset. There is an admission fee to enter the park during this period. However, visitors can still enjoy the park during the off-season by parking outside the gate and walking in during the same hours of operation. It's important to note that the park's facilities are closed during the off-season.

NOTES:

PASSPORT STAMPS

LILY BAY STATE PARK

COUNTY: PISCATAQUIS   ESTABLISHED: 1959   AREA (AC/HA): 925 / 374

DATE VISITED: LODGING: WHO I WENT WITH:

WEATHER: ☀☐ ☁☐ ☔☐ ❄☐ ⚡☐ 🌫☐   SPRING ☐ SUMMER ☐ FALL ☐ WINTER ☐

FEE(S):   RATING: ☆ ☆ ☆ ☆ ☆   WILL I RETURN? YES / NO

Lily Bay State Park, located on Moosehead Lake, offers picturesque waterfront camping and serves as the gateway to Maine's North Woods. This region is renowned for its abundance of outdoor recreational activities, ranging from hiking and canoeing to fishing and wildlife observation. The park was established in 1959, primarily using woodland that was generously donated to the State by the Scott Paper Company. Moosehead Lake, which spans an impressive 117 square miles, is the largest lake in New England. Its cool and clear waters, coupled with its relatively undeveloped shores, make it an enticing destination for boating enthusiasts, fishermen, and vacationers seeking a taste of wilderness. Covering an expansive 925 acres, Lily Bay State Park features two distinct camping areas that run along the lake, offering a total of 90 campsites. There is a dumping station, but there are no RV hookups. Campers have access to hot showers. There is one group site specifically for tent camping. Visitors can also enjoy a designated swimming beach, a playground, two trailerable boat ramps, and a scenic 2-mile walking trail that follows the shoreline. Moosehead Lake has cold water, and sudden winds can create hazardous conditions for small boats, causing waves up to 6 feet high. It is important to wear a personal flotation device (PFD) at all times, inform someone about your planned route and return time, and carefully monitor the conditions, especially when crossing open waters. Transporting firewood can introduce invasive insects and diseases that pose a threat to forests. Always obtain firewood from local sources. For more information, visit www.maine.gov/forestpests. Make sure to check yourself for deer ticks daily to prevent Lyme disease. Visitors are required to keep their pets on a leash at all times, with the leash length not exceeding 4 feet, and they should never leave their pets unattended. In the Moosehead region, boaters and campers enjoy the area during the warm months of the year. Following them, hunters visit in October and November, and in mid-winter, ice fishermen and snowmobilers take advantage of the region. The best time for fishing salmon and trout in Moosehead Lake is typically after the ice melts (usually early to mid-May) or when the water cools down in September. Anyone who wishes to fish, regardless of residency, must be at least 16 years old if they are Maine residents or 12 years old if they are non-residents. Additionally, they must possess a valid fishing license and familiarize themselves with the open water fishing regulations set by the State. Lily Bay State Park is open throughout the year from 9:00 a.m. until sunset, unless there are specific signs at the gate indicating otherwise. During the winter, the park staff maintains 5 miles of cross-country ski and snowshoe trails. It is advisable to make advance reservations for this popular campground. For more information or to make a reservation, please contact the State Park Reservations Office at 800-332-1501 (in

Maine) or 207-624-9950 (from outside Maine), or visit the website www.campwithme.com. Lily Bay State Park is located within The Maine Highlands Region, which encompasses notable attractions in the North Woods of Piscataquis and Somerset Counties, including Baxter State Park. Within an hour's drive of the park, there are several outdoor attractions worth exploring. Here are some highlights: Mt. Kineo: Situated at the heart of Moosehead Lake, Mt. Kineo is a remarkable landmark offering 5 miles of hiking trails and breathtaking summit views. Visitors can reach Kineo by taking a commercial boat shuttle from Rockwood. Prong Pond: This charming 427-acre pond is surrounded by small mountains and is a great spot for canoeing, kayaking, wildlife observation, and fishing. Access to the pond can be obtained through a trailerable boat launch. The narrow arms of the pond boast fascinating bog plants such as insect-eating sundews and pitcher plants. To reach the pond from the park, travel 1.6 miles to the right, then take a left onto the gravel Prong Pond Road. Finally, make an immediate right turn onto the road leading to the boat launch. Big Moose Mountain (3,196 feet): Located nearby, Big Moose Mountain offers an expansive and unobstructed summit view of the entire Moosehead region. The hike to the summit spans 3.75 miles and takes approximately 4 hours to complete. The trail gradually ascends to a fire warden's cabin and then becomes steeper leading to the summit. To reach the trailhead, travel west on Routes 6/15 from Greenville for about 4 miles and take a left onto North Road. After 1.2 miles, the trailhead will be on the right. Big Spencer Mountain (3,206 feet): The State owns the lands surrounding Big Spencer Mountain, maintaining the area as an Ecological Reserve. This challenging hike covers a rough 2-mile trail and takes approximately 3 hours roundtrip. The summit provides impressive views of Mt. Katahdin and the surrounding lakes. The final stretch of the hike involves a demanding ascent, including several ladders, with an elevation gain of a thousand feet over the last 0.7 miles. To access the trailhead, take a left from the Park and continue 8.3 miles past Kokadjo. Look for a dirt road on the left just after Bear Brook Campground. The trailhead will be on the left after 6.3 miles. Number 4 Mountain (2,890 feet): For a challenging hiking experience, travel 8.8 miles to the left from the Park and then turn right before reaching Kokadjo onto the Frenchtown Road (gravel). After 2.1 miles, make a right turn onto another gravel road. Proceed for 1.3 miles and then turn left onto another gravel road. After 0.9 miles, you will reach the trailhead on the left side (park 0.1 miles past the trailhead on the right). Lazy Tom Bog: To spot moose in their natural habitat, drive through Kokadjo until you reach the point where the road transitions to a dirt road. At this junction, take a left where you see a sign indicating Baxter State Park. Continue for 1.1 miles and then make a left turn at the sign directing you towards Spencer Pond Camps. Proceed for another 0.5 miles until you reach a small bridge. You can park your vehicle on either side of the bridge.

NOTES:

PASSPORT STAMPS

MACKWORTH ISLAND

COUNTY: CUMBERLAND **ESTABLISHED:** 1946 **AREA (AC/HA):** 100 / 40

DATE VISITED: **LODGING:** **WHO I WENT WITH:**

WEATHER: ☀️☐ ⛅☐ 🌧️☐ ❄️☐ ⛈️☐ 🌫️☐ SPRING ☐ SUMMER ☐ FALL ☐ WINTER ☐

FEE(S): **RATING:** ☆ ☆ ☆ ☆ ☆ **WILL I RETURN?** YES / NO

In 1946, Governor Percival Proctor Baxter generously donated Mackworth Island to the State of Maine, designating it for state public purposes and as a sanctuary for wildlife. The island received its name from Arthur Mackworth, to whom it was gifted by Sir Ferdinando Gorges, an early Maine colonizer, in 1631. Mackworth Island, a landmass of about 100 acres, is connected to Falmouth via a causeway located at the mouth of the Presumpscot River. This island's unique blend of human and natural history is a result of its close proximity to Portland and the Presumpscot. Although human activity has significantly impacted the island's natural environment, there is still much to appreciate and protect. The island is predominantly covered in dense woods, and a specific area within the woods is dedicated to "Fairy Houses," which visitors construct using natural materials found on the island. Mackworth Island boasts a picturesque rocky shoreline and presents ample opportunities for surf fishing, particularly for bluefish and stripers. The trail that encircles the island, spanning approximately 1 ¼ miles, can be leisurely completed in about an hour. Visitors will be rewarded with breathtaking views of Casco Bay and Portland. Along the trail, one can pause to observe boats and ferries navigating the Atlantic waters, while seagulls, osprey, and shorebirds gracefully soar above in search of food. The trail itself has a packed soil surface, which may become slippery when wet. The terrain is generally flat, with slopes not exceeding 10%. The main loop of the trail is wheelchair-accessible, as there are no steps or significant barriers, aside from rocks, roots, and a few waterbars. However, some of the smaller side trails leading down the steep slope towards the shore may be inaccessible to certain visitors. It is advisable to closely supervise children in areas with steep rocky terrain. Mackworth Island is home to the Governor Baxter School for the Deaf, which is not open to the general public unless prior arrangements have been made. Additionally, the island houses the Governor Baxter Dog Memorial, a pet cemetery where fourteen Irish Setters and one horse belonging to the former governor rest in peace. The memorial is adorned with two bronze markers, a gravestone, and enclosed by a circular stone wall.

NOTES:

PASSPORT STAMPS

MOOSE POINT STATE PARK

COUNTY: WALDO	ESTABLISHED: 1963	AREA (AC/HA): 146 / 59

DATE VISITED:　　**LODGING:**　　　**WHO I WENT WITH:**

WEATHER: ☀☐ ⛅☐ ❄☐ ❄☐ ⛈☐ 🌫☐　SPRING☐ SUMMER☐ FALL☐ WINTER☐

FEE(S):　　**RATING:** ☆ ☆ ☆ ☆ ☆　　**WILL I RETURN?** YES / NO

The park operates from 9:00 a.m. until sunset every day between Memorial Day and October 1st. During this period, visitors are required to pay an admission fee. However, even during the off-season, visitors are welcome to enjoy the park by parking their vehicles outside the gate without obstructing it and entering on foot within the same operating hours. In such cases, visitors are requested to deposit the admission fee in the self-service collection canister. It's important to note that park facilities are closed during the off-season. Visitors to Moose Point State Park can relax and enjoy the scenic view of Penobscot Bay. Positioned along US Route 1, Moose Point attracts many travelers exploring this scenic coastal route. Visitors can delight in the peaceful atmosphere of the evergreen grove, discover fascinating tidal pools, take a stroll along the park's trails, or simply bask in the beautiful vistas. This park is strictly designated for day-use activities, and camping facilities are not available. If you are interested in camping, the nearest State Park with camping options is located at Camden Hills State Park. Visitors are allowed to bring pets to the park, but they must be kept on a leash and under the direct supervision of their handlers. The group shelter and gazebo offer an idyllic waterfront location ideal for hosting weddings or family reunions. The shelter is furnished with four electrical outlets, a sink with running water, and ample picnic tables to comfortably accommodate up to 72 individuals. Additionally, the shelter's parking area can conveniently hold up to 30 vehicles. To secure a reservation for the Group Shelter & Gazebo, please contact the park directly at (207) 548-2882 during the months of April to October, or reach out to the Park Office at (207) 941-4014 from November to March. In most cases, weddings at the parks do not necessitate special permits. However, certain arrangements may require obtaining specific permissions. To ensure a smooth and delightful experience on your big day, it is advisable to plan your event well in advance and communicate closely with the Park Manager. Visitors are allowed to have catering services at the park, but it is important to remember that the park follow a Carry-In, Carry-Out policy. Whether you hire an external caterer or bring your own food, it is your responsibility to ensure that all trash is properly removed at the conclusion of the event. For specific inquiries regarding tents and other structures, it is recommended to consult with the park manager. The weather in Maine can be unpredictable, so it is crucial to have contingency plans in place, especially for outdoor weddings held at parks without group shelters.

NOTES:

PASSPORT STAMPS

MOUNT BLUE STATE PARK

COUNTY: FRANKLIN	ESTABLISHED: 1955	AREA (AC/HA): 7,489 / 3,030
DATE VISITED:	LODGING:	WHO I WENT WITH:
WEATHER: ☀☐ ☁☐ ☃☐ ❄☐ 🌧☐ 🌊☐		SPRING ☐ SUMMER ☐ FALL ☐ WINTER ☐
FEE(S):	RATING: ☆ ☆ ☆ ☆ ☆	WILL I RETURN? YES / NO

Spanning approximately 8,000 acres, Mount Blue State Park is the largest state park in Maine. It is divided into two sections, separated by Webb Lake. The Webb Beach section houses a campground with 136 wooded sites, just a short walk away from a sandy beach and picnic area. Visitors can enjoy swimming, boating (including rentals), and walking on the trails near the lake. During the summer months, park staff regularly organize canoe trips, guided walks, and nature programs. There is also a Nature Center with interactive exhibits and displays. Across the lake from the Webb Beach section lies the centerpiece of the park, Mount Blue, standing at an elevation of 3,187 feet. This peak is a popular choice for day-hikers. Additionally, visitors can partake in leisurely walks and picnics on Center Hill. The park offers 25 miles of challenging, multi-use trails for mountain bikers, equestrians, and ATV riders. In winter, the extensive trail system supports activities such as snowmobiling, snowshoeing, and cross-country skiing. Families are drawn to the park for sledding adventures on Center Hill and the chance to skate on an outdoor ice rink complete with a warming hut, located at the Center Hill Road Park Headquarters. Mount Blue State Park welcomes visitors throughout the year, remaining open year-round. The park's operating hours are from 9:00 a.m. until sunset, unless otherwise indicated at the entrance gate. The park may have earlier openings depending on the season, so it is advisable to call ahead and confirm these times, including the campground hours. An entry fee is collected year-round, either by park staff at the entry booth or through a self-service station. When bringing pets into the park, they must be leashed, attended to, and under control at all times. All trash must be carried out of the park. ATVs and snowmobiles are only allowed on designated trails. The park is conveniently located within a few hours' drive from several major cities. The park offers 136 campsites near Webb Lake, each equipped with a fireplace and picnic table. These sites can accommodate both tents and RVs. Some sites have electric and water hook-ups. An RV dumping station for campers is available. Large groups can reserve four designated sites. It is recommended to make advanced reservations for the campground, and you can do so by contacting the State Park Reservations Office at 800-332-1501 (within Maine) or 207-624-9950 (outside of Maine). Alternatively, you can make your own reservations online at www.campwithme.com. Please note that camping is not permitted on Tumbledown Public Land. Winter camping is available at the park from December 15 to March 15, but please note that it is primitive tent camping only. There are no amenities, cleared campsites, or maintained trails during this time. It is essential to have experience with winter camping and be self-sufficient. Access to the campsites is possible only by snowshoe or skis. When arriving, self-registration is required, and you can do so at the entry booth. Camping fees apply and should be paid during self-registration. Remember to carry out all your trash and leave no trace. For more information, you can visit the website www.maine.gov/dacf/parks/camping/off-season-camping.shtml or contact the park directly at (207) 585-2261. The park offers two picnic shelters that can be reserved for group gatherings. A waterfront picnic area is situated along Webb Lake.Another picnic area is located at the top of Center Hill. Services and facilities available at Mount Blue State Park also include: A playground for children to enjoy. Hot showers, flush and pit toilets, and changing facilities for swimmers. An amphitheater and nature center featuring interactive displays and exhibits. Rentals of rowboats, kayaks, paddle boats, paddle boards, and canoes (available during the summer season). Tumbledown Public Land, adjacent to Mt. Blue State Park, comprises over 22,000 acres of State-owned Public Lands and State-held easements that encompass the Tumbledown Mountain Range. While Tumbledown Mountain itself, featuring an alpine pond near its summit, is the most popular hiking destination, the surrounding lands offer a wide range of outdoor opportunities. This vast and undisturbed landscape serves as vital wildlife habitat while catering to human needs. Visitors to the area may have the chance to encounter moose, deer, and occasional sightings of bears, coyotes, or foxes. The diverse birdlife includes numerous songbirds, including all six species of thrush that breed in Maine. Hikers can explore various trails and peaks, many of which offer breathtaking panoramic views. The longstanding traditions of hunting and timber harvesting continue to this day, with a strong commitment to sustainable practices certified by recognized standards. Between 18,000 and 14,000 years ago, massive ice sheets extended across the region, leaving a lasting impact on the landscape. These ice sheets carved deep valleys, including the one where Webb Lake is located, and left their mark on exposed rocks. Indigenous communities later utilized this area for seasonal hunting and trapping, establishing permanent settlements near abundant food sources such as large lakes, rivers, and the coastal areas. The first farm in the region was established in 1798, and within three decades, a significant portion of the pristine forest covering the lower slopes was cleared. As the 1900s approached, numerous farms in the area were abandoned, and remnants of this era can still be discovered by visitors, such as stone walls and cellar holes that serve as reminders of the past. During the challenging period of the Great Depression in the 1930s, the federal government took action by acquiring 51 parcels of land that were considered marginal for farming. This initiative was carried out under the U.S. Resettlement Administration Land Utilization Project. To develop this land into what is now known as Mount Blue State Park, the federal Works Progress Administration employed workers and embarked on constructing essential infrastructure, including roads and buildings. The U.S. Department of Agriculture later transferred ownership of the property to the State in 1955. Over time, additional land acquisitions were made, expanding the park's boundaries to its present size of 8,000 acres. For many generations, traditional trails that extended beyond the boundaries of the park traversed private forest lands, posing a potential threat to access rights. Recognizing the importance of preserving these areas, various organizations and groups united their efforts to secure the summit and northern slopes of Tumbledown Mountain, the parcels adjacent to the Webb Beach Campground and East Brook, the entirety of Jackson Mountain, the peak of Blueberry Mountain, the entire Jackson Pond, and easements on an additional 12,000 acres of land. While certain sections of the public lands have experienced timber harvesting, with some occurring shortly before the State's acquisition, there are still pockets of wooded areas that have seen minimal cutting and harbor hardwood trees that are over 150 years old. Presently, the forests within Tumbledown Public Land are subject to scientific and sustainable management practices to ensure their long-term preservation. Hiking Trails at Mount Blue State Park: Mt. Blue Trail: This trail is approximately 3.2 miles roundtrip and takes about 3-4 hours to complete. It is rated as moderate to difficult and offers stunning scenic vistas and an observation tower at the peak. Birdwatching opportunities and vibrant wildflowers can be enjoyed along the trail. At the summit, there is an observation deck for visitors to take in the panoramic views. Center Hill Nature Trail: This trail is an easy 0.5-mile roundtrip hike that takes about 1 hour to complete. It features numbered way stations and an interpretive brochure, allowing visitors to learn more about the cultural and natural history of the region. The trail begins at the parking lot of the Center Hill picnic area. Campground Trails: These trails can be accessed by traveling 2.4 miles north on Route 142, passing Weld Village, and then taking a left onto West Side Road at Webb Corner. Continue for 4 miles until you reach Webb Beach Road, which leads to the lake and campground at 187 Webb Beach Road. Hopping Frog Nature Trail: This trail is a 1-mile roundtrip hike that takes about 1 hour to complete. A self-guided brochure is available at the trailhead. The trail follows a meandering path along the shore of Webb Lake and Swett Brook, offering an ideal setting for nature study. It starts near the Park's nature center and follows the same route back. Swett Brook Trail: This trail forms a 2-mile loop that takes about 2 hours to complete and is rated as easy to moderate. It encircles the upland forest surrounding the Webb Lake campground, providing a great opportunity for exercise and family nature walks. To access the trailheads for Tumbledown, with the exception of Blueberry Mountain, you can take the Byron Road, which intersects with the West Side Road about a quarter-mile west of Webb Corner. The West Side Road can be reached by traveling 2.4 miles north of Weld Village on Route 142. Loop Trail - Tumbledown Mountain (various roundtrip options, 4-5 hours, challenging): The Loop Trail is one of the more demanding routes to Tumbledown Mountain. It involves a steep ascent of 1.5 miles to a trail juncture. From there, you can take the 0.2-mile Tumbledown Mountain Trail, which leads to the summit. Alternatively, you can descend over the open ridgeline for 0.6 miles to Tumbledown Pond. From Tumbledown Pond, it is possible to continue hiking down the Brook Trail for 1.8 miles and then head west on the Byron Road for a little over 1.25 miles to return to the starting point. The trailhead for the Loop Trail is located 5.5 miles from the beginning of the Byron Road. Brook Trail (3 miles roundtrip, 3 hours, moderate): The Brook Trail follows the path of Tumbledown Brook and offers the most direct and efficient route to Tumbledown Pond. The trail concludes at the alpine pond where it intersects with the Loop Trail, Parker Ridge Trail, and Pond Link

Trail. The trailhead for the Brook Trail can be found 3.7 miles from the eastern end of Byron Road, near a large parking area just uphill from a brook crossing. Parker Ridge Trail (5.8 miles roundtrip, 5 hours, moderate): To access the Parker Ridge Trail, take a cutoff from the beginning of the Brook Trail. The one-mile Little Jackson Connector trail features gentle terrain and connects with the 1.8-mile Parker Ridge Trail. This trail offers a picturesque path to Tumbledown Pond, including a segment along an open ridge with expansive views. Little Jackson Mountain Trail (7 miles roundtrip, 6 hours, challenging): For those seeking a challenging hike with excellent birdwatching opportunities, scenic brooks, and magnificent views, the Little Jackson Mountain Trail is an ideal choice. To access this trail, take the Little Jackson Connector trail from the beginning of the Brook Trail. Follow the connector trail for 1.1 miles and then veer right after passing the junction of the Parker Ridge Trail. Look for the Little Jackson Mountain Trail on your left. Pond Link Trail (1.1 miles one-way, 1 hour, moderate): The Pond Link Trail serves as a connection between Tumbledown Pond and the Little Jackson Trail. This trail segment allows for loop hikes using either the Little Jackson Trail and the Brook Trail or the Loop Trail. It spans a distance of 1.1 miles and provides a moderate hiking experience. Blueberry Mountain Trail (2.2 miles roundtrip, 3 hours, moderate): The Blueberry Mountain Trail commences behind the Blueberry Mountain Bible Camp, which is accessible via a 2-mile dirt road off Route 142. This trail features steep sections, particularly near the beginning, but overall offers a moderately challenging hike with rewarding panoramic views. Please be mindful of the private land that the trail traverses and park your vehicle in the designated parking lot before the camp lodge, rather than at the sports field beyond. Multi-use Trails: The multi-use trail network spans approximately 18 miles, starting from the park headquarters and connecting to the State-wide interconnected trail system in Phillips. Whether you're exploring on a mountain bike, ATV, horseback, or on foot, you'll encounter diverse terrain, including old unimproved roads and wooded sections that provide exciting riding experiences. To access these trails, follow Center Hill Road from Weld Village until you reach the park headquarters, which offers ample parking. For statewide ATV and multi-use trail information, visit www.parksandlands.com or call (207) 287-2751. Winter Trails: During the winter season, Mount Blue State Park offers cross-country ski trails that allow visitors to explore the park's more remote areas amidst the splendor of winter. Six trails traverse through forests, fields, and old farmlands, providing a range of scenic experiences. With a total length of fifteen miles, these ski trails feature set tracks and vary in distance from half a mile to ten miles. Snowmobile trails are also available, winding through the park and connecting to the Maine ITS (Interconnected Trail System) and local trails. For more information about snowmobiling and the ITS system, you can visit www.parksandlands.com or call (207) 287-4957. Please take note of the following important considerations: Be prepared for weather changes by wearing suitable footwear and layered clothing. Carry windproof and waterproof clothing. Inform someone about your planned destination and expected return time. Only purchase local firewood and ensure that boats and motors are thoroughly cleaned to prevent the introduction of invasive plants and animals. For more information, visit www.maine.gov/firewood and www.maine.gov/dep/water/invasives. Avoid leaving valuables unattended in your vehicle. Stay on established trails, even if they are muddy, to protect sensitive ecosystems, especially in summit areas. Observe wildlife from a distance that does not disturb their behavior. Refrain from following or feeding animals. Avoid areas with nesting birds, dens, or young animals, even if they appear abandoned. Be prepared for black flies and mosquitoes, especially in May and June. Although the area is not heavily infested with deer ticks, it is still advisable to check yourself daily to prevent Lyme disease. Do not solely rely on your cell phone in case of an emergency, as coverage in the area may be limited or non-existent. Vehicle GPS systems may be unreliable in this region. Baiting wildlife for hunting is prohibited at Mount Blue State Park. Trapping may be allowed with written permission from the Bureau if it is within the State Park and complies with local ordinances and the laws and rules of the Maine Department of Inland Fisheries and Wildlife. For more information, visit www.maine.gov/ifw. In the vicinity of Mt. Blue State Park and the Tumbledown Range, you will find several nearby destinations worth exploring. This area is part of Maine's Lakes and Mountains Region, which includes Franklin and Oxford Counties and represents the westernmost portion of the state. Here are some nearby destinations: Androscoggin Riverlands State Park: Located just north of Lewiston-Auburn, this expansive 2,800-acre park boasts 12 miles of river frontage. It offers abundant opportunities for walking, fishing, boating, wildlife watching, and hunting. Grafton Notch State Park/Mahoosuc Public Lands: This mountainous region spans 33,000 acres and features breathtaking scenery, including numerous waterfalls and gorges. Visitors can enjoy hiking, picnicking, and sightseeing in this area known for its natural beauty. Rangeley Lake State Park: Situated in the heart of Maine's Western Mountains, this park covers 869 acres. It offers 50 campsites along the shores of cool, clear waters, which are perfect for boating and fishing enthusiasts. Kennebec Highlands: Located west of Augusta in the Belgrade Lakes region, the Kennebec Highlands encompasses over 15,000 acres of conserved lands. This area provides a wide range of recreational opportunities and is protected through a public-private partnership. Interesting places located near the park: Height of Land: This famous overlook is located on Route 17 between Byron and Rangeley. It offers a breathtaking vista of the entire Rangeley region and provides access to the Appalachian Trail. Visitors can enjoy stunning views and immerse themselves in the natural beauty of the area. Coos Canyon: Situated in Byron, Coos Canyon is a picturesque gorge along the Swift River. It offers not only scenic beauty but also an opportunity for gold panning. Visitors can try their luck at finding gold and enjoy swimming in the crystal-clear waters of this spectacular natural setting. Smalls Falls Rest Area: Located just south of Rangeley on Route 4, the Smalls Falls Rest Area is a delightful spot for a picnic and swimming. It features a cascading set of falls within a scenic gorge along the Sandy River. Visitors can relax, enjoy a meal, and take a refreshing dip in the swimming hole while surrounded by the beauty of nature. State Route 27: Designated as a National Scenic Byway, State Route 27 runs from Kingfield north through the Carrabassett Valley all the way to the Canadian border. This scenic route offers stunning views and takes travelers through beautiful landscapes. It is an ideal choice for those seeking a scenic drive and an opportunity to appreciate the natural splendor of the region.

NOTES:

PASSPORT STAMPS

MOUNT KINEO STATE PARK

COUNTY: PISCATAQUIS	ESTABLISHED: -	AREA (AC/HA): 800 / 323

DATE VISITED:	LODGING:	WHO I WENT WITH:

WEATHER: ☀☐ ☁☐ ☷☐ ❄☐ ☔☐ ☁☐	SPRING ☐ SUMMER ☐ FALL ☐ WINTER ☐

FEE(S):	RATING: ☆ ☆ ☆ ☆ ☆	WILL I RETURN? YES / NO

Standing tall at an elevation of 1,789 feet, Mount Kineo commands the landscape of Moosehead Lake. Its cliff face rises dramatically, towering 700 feet above the lake's surface and providing crucial habitat for rare plant species and peregrine falcons. To reach Mount Kineo, there is no road access available. Visitors can instead access the park by boat, departing from the public access site located in Rockwood. During the summer months, there is a commercial shuttle service available for transportation. The Mount Kineo Golf Course operates a seasonal water shuttle service from the public dock in Rockwood to Mount Kineo. It is believed to be the second oldest golf course in New England and has been under new ownership since 2009. The course retains its original 1893 layout and features a classic lakeside design with no sand traps and small greens. One of the standout holes is the par 3 hole #4, which offers scenic views over the water with the impressive backdrop of the Kineo cliff. Open year-round, Mount Kineo welcomes visitors from 9:00 a.m. until sunset each day, unless otherwise indicated at the gate. A fee is charged for entry. The park provides a variety of activities for visitors to enjoy, including birdwatching, boating (motorized), fishing, and hiking. When hiking on any of the trails, it is recommended to wear sturdy footwear that provides good grip and support. Additionally, it is essential to carry an ample water supply and extra layers of clothing to prepare for changing weather conditions. Exercise caution when near cliffs, especially when the surroundings are damp and slippery, to ensure personal safety. Moosehead Lake is known for its cold water, and it's important to be aware that winds can quickly pick up, creating hazardous conditions for boaters. According to the law, children who are 10 years old and younger must wear a Type I, II, or III personal flotation device (PFD) while on any watercraft. It is recommended that all boaters, regardless of age, wear a PFD at all times when in small boats. Before heading out, inform someone about your planned route and estimated return time. Stay vigilant of the weather conditions, especially when crossing open waters, including the route to Mount Kineo. The Maine Department of Inland Fisheries and Wildlife (MDIFW) Warden Service is responsible for conducting search-and-rescue operations and enforcing state fish and game laws, boating laws on inland waters, as well as ATV and snowmobile laws. For more information about these laws and to purchase the appropriate licenses, you can visit the official website at www.maine.gov/ifw. When it comes to firewood, it is recommended to buy it locally and follow the "Burn It Where You Buy It" principle. Additionally, it is crucial to thoroughly clean boats and motors to prevent the introduction of invasive plant and animal species. In emergency situations, relying solely on your cell phone may not be reliable due to limited or no coverage in certain areas. The region is home to abundant wildlife such as moose, bears, and other large animals. It is important to exercise caution when encountering them. Drive at a slow speed on area roads, especially during low-light conditions, and maintain a safe distance when observing wildlife. When camping, store food items securely and ensure that tents and their contents are free of any food or food odors. Be cautious while traveling on logging roads, yield and stop for trucks regardless of their direction. Avoid narrow roads that cannot accommodate two vehicles, refrain from blocking side roads, and avoid stopping in areas with poor visibility. Keep in mind that roads can be dusty in dry weather and prone to washouts during wet weather. Travel at a slow speed on gravel roads to minimize wear on tires and suspension systems, and always carry a spare tire. Mount Kineo is located in the Maine Highlands Region, which includes Baxter State Park and other notable attractions in Piscataquis and Somerset Counties. Here are some nearby destinations: Moosehead Lake Public Land. Moosehead Lake, the largest freshwater body in New England, is situated at the entrance to the North Maine Woods. It provides opportunities for camping, fishing, hunting, paddling, hiking, snowmobiling, and cross-country skiing. The majestic cliffs of Mount Kineo, towering 700 feet above the lake, create a stunning landscape that has long been appreciated for its natural beauty and abundant resources. Lily Bay State Park: Located nine miles north of Greenville, Lily Bay State Park offers 91 campsites nestled in a wooded and lakeside setting. The park spans 925 acres along the shores of Moosehead Lake and features two boat launches. It is a picturesque location for camping and enjoying various recreational activities. Native Americans used to travel long distances to Mt. Kineo to obtain its rhyolite rock, which is one of the largest formations of its kind in the world. This rhyolite, along with slate and sandstone, reveals the mountain's geological history, including volcanic, sedimentary, and metaphoric phases. The rhyolite on Mount Kineo has properties similar to flint and was extensively used by indigenous peoples to create arrowheads and tools. It is often referred to as "Kineo flint" in literature, but this term is misleading as it implies a sedimentary origin, while the rhyolite is actually an igneous extrusive material formed during volcanic activity. As the largest known deposit of this rock in the country, it was sought after by indigenous people for centuries, and their implements made from this stone have been found throughout New England and even further south. In 1846, Henry David Thoreau visited the Moosehead Lake region and was deeply interested in the geological formation of Mt. Kineo, as well as the Indian relics and traditions associated with it. The first Mt. Kineo House, a hotel resort, was built on the shores of Moosehead Lake in 1848 but was destroyed by fire in 1868. It was rebuilt in 1870 and opened in 1871, only to be burned down again in 1882. The third iteration of the hotel, designed by Arthur H. Vinal, opened in 1884. In 1911, the Maine Central Railroad purchased the resort and operated it through the Hiram Ricker Hotel Company. It was the largest inland waterfront hotel in America at the time, accommodating over 500 guests. However, the railroad discontinued its Kineo branch in 1933 and sold the hotel in 1938. During the demolition process, the hotel burned down, and in 2018, the old employee house also suffered the same fate.

NOTES:

PASSPORT STAMPS

OWLS HEAD LIGHT STATE PARK

COUNTY: KNOX	ESTABLISHED: 1978	AREA (AC/HA): 13 / 5.2

DATE VISITED: **LODGING:**   **WHO I WENT WITH:**

WEATHER: ☀☐ ☁☐ ☂☐ ❄☐ ⚡☐ 🌫☐   SPRING☐ SUMMER☐ FALL☐ WINTER☐

FEE(S):   **RATING:** ☆ ☆ ☆ ☆ ☆   **WILL I RETURN?** YES / NO

Owls Head Light, situated at the entrance of Rockland Harbor on the western side of Penobscot Bay in Owls Head, Maine, is an active navigational aid. The lighthouse is under the ownership of the U.S. Coast Guard and licensed to the American Lighthouse Foundation. It stands as the focal point of Owls Head State Park, occupying a 13-acre area, and holds a place on the National Register of Historic Places as Owls Head Light Station since 1978. The town of Owls Head is located south of Rockland and features a peninsula that extends northeast into Penobscot Bay, with its tip lying east of downtown Rockland. Positioned at the eastern tip of this peninsula is the light station. Originally established in 1825, the light station was constructed with a round tower made of rubblestone by Jeremiah Berry, Green & Foster. The tower was later rebuilt in 1852, presenting a cylindrical brick structure standing on top of a granite foundation, measuring 30 feet in height. Perched on a cliff, it boasts one of the six remaining operational Fresnel lenses in Maine and stands 100 feet above mean sea level. In 1854, a separate keeper's house was built near the lighthouse. This cottage now serves as the headquarters for the American Lighthouse Foundation. A fourth-order Fresnel lens was installed in 1856, while additional structures, including a generator house and an oil storage building, were added in 1895. Renovations took place in 2010, aiming to restore the tower's appearance to its original state from 1852. The restoration project involved repainting the tower, repairing the bricks, ironwork, and windowpanes of the lantern, as well as the floor of the parapet. However, visitors are allowed to park at the designated parking lot and enjoy the amenities such as the picnic grove. They can also take a stroll either to the small rocky beach, which offers views of Rockland, or near the lighthouse grounds and the lighthouse itself, situated on the bluff above. The park provides picnic tables for visitors to enjoy outdoor meals and offers access to the shore for recreational activities. The park is open year-round and operates from 9:00 a.m. until sunset every day. There are no fees charged for entry at this location. Camden Hills State Park, located in the vicinity, offers a range of attractions for visitors to enjoy. The park is known for its scenic beauty and panoramic views of the surrounding area. It encompasses the Camden Hills, a prominent mountain range that rises above the coastal town of Camden, Maine.

NOTES:

PASSPORT STAMPS

PEAKS-KENNY STATE PARK

COUNTY: PISCATAQUIS	ESTABLISHED: 1969	AREA (AC/HA): 839 / 339

DATE VISITED: LODGING: WHO I WENT WITH:

WEATHER: ☀☐ ☁☐ 🌧☐ ❄☐ ⛈☐ 🌬☐ SPRING☐ SUMMER☐ FALL☐ WINTER☐

FEE(S): RATING: ☆ ☆ ☆ ☆ ☆ WILL I RETURN? YES / NO

Peaks-Kenny State Park is situated on the scenic shores of Sebec Lake, providing a serene and wooded environment for both day visitors and campers. It offers a range of recreational activities, including boating, fishing, swimming, hiking, and picnicking. The campground, nestled among majestic trees and large glacial boulders near the lake, encourages a peaceful and private experience amidst the beauty of nature. Spanning across 839 acres, the park is located in the Central Maine Highlands, a region renowned for its natural splendor and abundant outdoor opportunities. Within a short drive, visitors can explore attractions like Moosehead Lake, the Appalachian Trail, the southern section of Baxter State Park, and other outdoor destinations. During the warmer months, the Sebec Lake region attracts boaters and campers. Following them, in October and November, hunters take to the area, and in mid-winter, ice fishermen and snowmobilers arrive. The best time for salmon and trout fishing in Sebec Lake is typically after the ice melts (usually early to mid-May) or when the waters cool down in September. The park boasts over a mile of shoreline along Sebec Lake, with a sandy swimming beach that offers breathtaking views of Borestone Mountain. During the summer months, the beach is supervised by a lifeguard, ensuring a safe and enjoyable swimming experience. Adjacent to the beach, there is a grassy picnic area equipped with playground facilities, complete with tables and barbecue grills. This area is enjoyed by both campers and day visitors alike. The campground is conveniently located just a five-minute walk away from the beach, and it features numerous glacial boulders that children visiting the park love to climb. There are a total of 56 individual campsites spread out in a wooded area, ensuring privacy and a peaceful camping experience. For convenience, there is a trailer dump station for campers. The day use area offers 50 picnic sites equipped with grills for outdoor cooking. There is a designated handicap-accessible picnic site and campsite, ensuring accessibility for all visitors. A pavilion is available for group use. A sandy beach is available for swimming, with lifeguards present during the summer season. Canoe rentals are also offered for those who want to explore the water. A playground area with equipment is available for children to enjoy. The park presents visitors with a network of hiking trails spanning 10 miles, with some trails interconnected. The Cove Trail, measuring 0.7 miles, commences from the beach picnic area and offers a brief loop through the wooded area. For those desiring a swift immersion in the woods, the Loop Trail covers 0.5 miles and provides a conveniently located loop. The Birch Mountain Ledge Trail, a roundtrip of 2 miles, meanders through a mature forest, leading hikers to ledges atop Birch Mountain. For a more demanding hiking experience encompassing diverse forested landscapes, the Brown's Point Trail spans a distance of 5.5 miles roundtrip and typically requires around 2 hours to complete. Approximately 15,000 years ago, a massive ice sheet covered the state of Maine, carving out the basin where Sebec Lake now exists. The entire region was transformed by the mile-thick ice sheet, which removed most of the soil and exposed the underlying bedrock, creating a deep bowl that eventually became the lake. Shortly after the glaciers receded around 11,000 years ago, the first Paleo Indians arrived in the area, although there is limited evidence of their temporary encampments. However, artifacts from the Archaic period (4,000 to 9,000 years ago) shed light on the habits of the native people during that time. They camped along the shores of lakes and rivers, hunting deer, trapping fur-bearing animals, and catching shad and salmon using fish weirs. Initially, they used dugout canoes, but approximately 3,000 years ago, they started utilizing birch bark for various purposes such as baskets, houses, buckets, and canoes. In the early 1800s, European settlers arrived in the area, primarily working in the logging industry. The abundant timber resources were harvested for shipbuilding and later supplied lumber mills and paper mills. Steamboats were used to transport logs across the lake. A spool mill, slate quarry, and fish hatchery also briefly operated in the vicinity. Eventually, these industries gave way to sporting camps and a few summer camps, attracting visitors who enjoyed fishing, picnicking, and exploring ice caves and local mountains. A notable landmark on the lake is the "Castle," a shorefront home constructed in 1890 by a lawyer from Foxcroft who was inspired by European castles. This individual later became Maine's first Commissioner of Inland Fisheries and Game, implementing conservation measures such as a single deer limit and state fishing licenses. The portions of Peaks-Kenny State Park that are now developed were donated to the State in 1964 by Francis J. Peaks, a respected citizen and lawyer from Dover-Foxcroft. Francis Peaks, who had served in the Maine House of Representatives, generously gifted this picturesque recreational area to the State. The park includes a stunning white sand beach located at Sand Cove, which had long been a beloved spot for picnicking. Francis made this donation in loving memory of his sister, Annie Peaks Kenny, as well as their parents, Joseph and Eliza Peaks, who are honored through the park's name. Peaks-Kenny State Park officially opened its doors to the public on July 4, 1969. To ensure the protection of Maine's inland waters, all motorized boats must obtain and display a Lake and River Protection Sticker. The funds generated from these stickers contribute to efforts aimed at preventing and monitoring the spread of aquatic invasive species. If you are bringing a boat on a trailer, it is essential to ensure that your boat, propeller, trailer, anchor, and fishing gear are free of weeds before launching. This precaution helps prevent the introduction and spread of invasive plants such as Eurasian milfoil. If you come across any plants, please dispose of them on high, dry ground or in the trash. If you plan to engage in fishing activities, it is necessary for individuals aged 16 and above (Maine residents) or 12 and above (non-residents) to have a valid fishing license. Make sure to review the State's regulations regarding open water fishing. To protect the well-being of loons, eagles, and other wildlife, fishermen are encouraged to use lead-free sinkers and jigs to avoid metal poisoning. Fishing licenses can be obtained online or purchased at local sporting goods stores, convenience stores, or the Dover-Foxcroft Town Office. It is important to note that Maine has issued a freshwater fish consumption advisory due to the presence of mercury, which enters waterways through airborne pollution and accumulates in fish, posing significant health risks. The State has set strict limits on the recommended consumption of freshwater fish. For detailed information, please refer to the open water fishing regulations. Whether you are boating or hiking, it is crucial to be prepared. Bring extra clothing, including appropriate footwear, as well as a map and compass. Make sure to have an adequate supply of water and food. Always inform someone about your planned destination and expected return time. Be aware that black flies and mosquitoes can be particularly prevalent in May and June. Take precautions by protecting yourself against these insects. Additionally, check yourself daily for deer ticks to prevent Lyme disease. Transporting firewood can unintentionally introduce exotic insects and diseases that pose a serious threat to our forests. To mitigate this risk, it is strongly advised not to transport firewood. Instead, purchase firewood from local sources and burn it at the location where it was purchased ("Burn It Where You Buy It" principle). Peaks-Kenny State Park is located in the Maine Highlands Region, which also encompasses other notable attractions in the North Woods, including Baxter State Park. Here are some highlights: Seboeis Public Lands cover an expansive area of 13,000 acres and are situated along the borders of two lakes. This picturesque location offers opportunities for camping, boating, fishing, and stunning views of Mt. Katahdin. Katahdin Iron Works State Historical Site showcases the remnants of a blast furnace and charcoal kiln, serving as silent witnesses to the once-thriving Katahdin Iron Works. From 1843 to 1890, these structures buzzed with activity, representing Maine's sole iron works operation in the nineteenth century. Gulf Hagas, designated as a National Natural Landmark, presents hikers with exhilarating and demanding trails. Located just west of Katahdin Iron Works, this area is renowned for its impressive gorge and offers a memorable outdoor experience.

NOTES:

PASSPORT STAMPS

PENOBSCOT NARROWS OBSERVATORY

COUNTY: HANCOCK	ESTABLISHED: 1931	AREA (AC/HA): - / -
DATE VISITED:	LODGING:	WHO I WENT WITH:
WEATHER: ☀☐ ☁☐ ☷☐ ❄☐ ⛆☐ ☁☐		SPRING ☐ SUMMER ☐ FALL ☐ WINTER ☐
FEE(S):	RATING: ☆ ☆ ☆ ☆ ☆	WILL I RETURN? YES / NO

The approval of the Penobscot Narrows Bridge and Observatory project took place in 2003, prompted by the discovery and evaluation of structural issues found on the 1931 Waldo-Hancock Bridge. In response, the Maine Department of Transportation organized a series of community meetings to discuss the problems and explore potential solutions. Consequently, an ambitious undertaking was initiated to design and construct a replacement bridge, aiming to have it fully operational within a remarkably tight timeframe of 41 months. The design of the Penobscot Narrows Bridge and Observatory skillfully blends elements from the past, present, and future. The bridge's pylons exhibit an obelisk design, reminiscent of historical granite monuments such as the Washington Monument (which, interestingly, shares the same granite used at Fort Knox). Utilizing a single-plane, cable-stayed design, the bridge represents an improvement over the cable suspension concept employed in the previous Waldo-Hancock Bridge. In this design, each cable supporting the bridge can be independently monitored and, if necessary, replaced throughout the bridge's lifespan. As the first and only cable-stayed bridge in Maine, and the sole bridge on the American continent featuring an observatory, the Penobscot Narrows Bridge and Observatory establishes a new benchmark for transportation structures. It successfully integrates its primary function with the life, history, and recreational aspects of the communities in which it resides. A quick one-minute elevator ride will transport you to one of the most extraordinary viewpoints in Maine. From a height of 420 feet above the Penobscot River, just a few miles from Penobscot Bay, you can enjoy a panoramic 360-degree view. This unique vantage point is situated atop the northern tower, also known as the "pylon," of the new Penobscot Narrows Bridge. Visitors to the observatory are treated to breathtaking sights of mountains, lakes, and portions of Penobscot Bay. If you direct your gaze downward, you'll see the river upon which the intrepid explorer Samuel de Champlain sailed in 1604. It was also the site of the Penobscot Expedition of 1779, where the American navy suffered its most devastating defeat, with 37 vessels burned and sunk. The observatory is situated on the grounds of Fort Knox, a third-system granite fortress constructed to prevent any future naval disasters on the Penobscot. To access the top of the tower, tickets can be purchased at the welcome station upon entering Fort Knox. Bridge and Observatory Facts: It is the only bridge in North and South America that features an observatory. In fact, there are only three such bridges worldwide, with the other two located in Thailand and Slovakia. The bridge incorporates an innovative nitrogen gas protection and monitoring system, which effectively prevents corrosion caused by moisture or other potentially corrosive elements on the cables. The cables are composed of approximately 331 miles of epoxy-covered strands, roughly equivalent to the distance between Portland and Fort Kent. The foundations of the bridge contain enough concrete to fill a football field that is 19 feet high. The reinforcing steel rods used in the bridge piers and towers weigh a total of 1.02 million pounds. The total weight of the bridge is approximately 10,500 African elephants, equivalent to roughly 126 million pounds. The bridge spans a length of 2,120 feet. To create the new Route 1, around 340,000 tons of rock were blasted from the Prospect side. The observatory is situated 42 stories above the river, offering an incredible view. The observatory elevator holds the distinction of being the tallest and fastest in the State of Maine.

NOTES:

PASSPORT STAMPS

PENOBSCOT RIVER CORRIDOR

COUNTY: PENOBSCOT	ESTABLISHED: -		AREA (AC/HA): - / -
DATE VISITED:	LODGING:	WHO I WENT WITH:	
WEATHER: ☀️☐ ☁️☐ 🌧️☐ ❄️☐ ⛅☐ 🌫️☐		SPRING ☐ SUMMER ☐ FALL ☐ WINTER ☐	
FEE(S):	RATING: ☆ ☆ ☆ ☆ ☆	WILL I RETURN? YES / NO	

The upper section of the Penobscot River flows through a landscape of mountains and forests, dominated by the imposing presence of Mt. Katahdin, the highest peak in Maine at 5,267 feet. This area offers abundant recreational opportunities and is steeped in local traditions. The Penobscot River Corridor (PRC) stretches over 100 miles, encompassing rivers and lakes, and provides more than 120 campsites for outdoor enthusiasts. It is renowned for its excellent fishing, canoeing, and thrilling whitewater paddling experiences. The region is teeming with wildlife, and visitors often have the chance to observe moose, deer, black bears, and bald eagles in their natural habitats. The PRC is divided into four distinct areas: the Seboomook/Canada Falls area, the Upper West Branch and Lobster Lake, Chesuncook Lake, and the Lower West Branch. The Canada Falls Area and Seboomook, encompassing approximately 41,436 acres of rolling hills and forests, are managed for recreational activities, wildlife preservation, and timber resources. This remote region provides numerous opportunities for outdoor enthusiasts, including hunting for deer, moose, bear, grouse, and woodcock. Fishing is also popular, with opportunities to catch wild brook trout and landlocked salmon. Boating, wildlife observation, and challenging whitewater paddling experiences can be enjoyed in this area. During the months of July through September, weekly releases from the dam below Canada Falls Lake create 3.5 miles of technically demanding Class IV to Class V whitewater. This scenic section of the river offers thrilling adventures for experienced paddlers. The flow of water below the Seboomook Lake Dam ensures good conditions for whitewater boating, with a series of gentle drops known as the Roll Dams, which are valued as a training area and also utilized for commercial excursions. Primitive campsites are situated along the rivers and lakes, providing excellent opportunities for family camping and serving as base camps for boating and fishing expeditions. Additionally, there are two private establishments within the area: Historic Pittston Farm and Seboomook Wilderness Campground. These accommodations offer lodging options for those seeking less rustic accommodations. Both establishments attract hunters during the fall season, while Pittston Farm also caters to snowmobilers on the "Moosehead Loop" trail and ATV enthusiasts who can access the farm from regional ATV trail networks on private land. The Upper West Branch and Lobster Lake area is the most rugged and untouched section of the Penobscot River Corridor. It provides a picturesque setting for canoeing, camping, and fishing, with calm waters extending from Roll Dam to Chesuncook Lake. Lobster Lake boasts mostly wooded shores, interspersed with sandy beaches and rocky formations. The lake showcases a mix of sedimentary and volcanic formations that contain a wealth of fossils. Visitors to this area delight in observing the abundant birdlife, fishing for landlocked salmon and trout, and embarking on hikes up Lobster Mountain from Jackson Cove. Chesuncook Lake, the third-largest lake in Maine, is a popular destination for fishing enthusiasts. Anglers flock here in search of salmon, brook trout, lake trout, white perch, and yellow perch. The lake offers stunning views of Mt. Katahdin and serves as a gateway to historic Chesuncook Village, which was recognized as a National Historic Landmark in 1973. Gero Island, located just across from the Village, has been designated as a State Ecological Reserve. It serves as a protected area where forest ecosystems are maintained in their natural state and carefully monitored over time. As the Penobscot River flows downstream from Chesuncook Lake, it enters the breathtaking Ripogenous Gorge, a two-mile-long canyon with towering granite walls. This gorge is known for its exhilarating and demanding whitewater, making it one of the most challenging high-volume whitewater destinations in the Northeast. The popular West Branch rafting trip commences at McKay Station, traverses the Gorge, and covers a total of 9 miles, combining sections of both flatwater and whitewater. Between Big Eddy and Ambejejus Lake, the river alternates between calm stretches of flat water and sections with rapids and waterfalls. These areas present exciting challenges for paddlers. Beyond Debsconeag Falls, the river gradually becomes calmer, and picturesque beaches emerge. Omaha Beach is a particularly popular spot for swimming, picnicking, and camping. The Lower West Branch offers a variety of campsites that are easily accessible by car or short walks. Some sites are specifically designated for tents, while others can accommodate large RVs. These camping areas provide convenient options for visitors to enjoy the natural beauty of the river. To ensure the preservation of the river corridor, the state holds a conservation easement on privately owned timberlands along the river. This permanent legal agreement restricts development within 500 feet of the water's edge and grants the Bureau of Parks and Lands the authority to manage the river for public recreational use. For nearly 12,000 years, the rivers, streams, and lakes in the Seboomook/Penobscot region have served as vital pathways for the native people who inhabited this area. Canoe routes have existed here for at least 1,000 years, connecting the Kennebec, Penobscot, and Allagash rivers. These historic routes continue to be enjoyed by modern recreational paddlers who traverse the 740-mile Northern Forest Canoe Trail. Renowned writer and naturalist Henry David Thoreau explored some of these waterways during his three extended trips between 1846 and 1857. His book, "The Maine Woods," vividly depicts his journeys through the untamed landscapes that attracted both adventurers and lumbermen. During Thoreau's time, logging activities had already begun in the region and continued to expand throughout the 19th century. The Great Northern Paper Company, which was established during Thoreau's era, operated two local establishments near Seboomook Lake. These facilities provided accommodations and meals for lumbermen and passing sportsmen. In 1906, the company acquired Pittston Farm and the surrounding township. At its peak, the farm had over 100 horses and a boarding house capable of accommodating 40 people. The Great Northern Paper Company also managed another property known as the Seboomook House, which is now the location of the Seboomook Wilderness Campground. During World War II, the federal government utilized this property as an internment camp for approximately 200 to 250 German and Czech prisoners of war. These prisoners were assigned daily tasks of cutting pulpwood with axes and saws as part of their internment. Over the course of many years, numerous dams were constructed throughout the river corridor to facilitate log floating and provide power for sawmills and later paper mills. Among these dams, Seboomook and Canada Falls Lakes were formed. Currently, both dams are under the ownership of Great Lakes Hydro America LLC and operate as part of a headwaters storage system that contributes to the generation of hydropower downstream. Ripogenus Dam, considered the largest privately built dam at the time of its construction, merged three preexisting lakes to form Chesuncook Lake. The small logging settlement of Chesuncook Village, located in close proximity, was designated as a National Historic Landmark in 1973. While only a few individuals reside in the village year-round, it is home to Chesuncook Lake House, an inn established in 1864 to cater to the needs of the region's loggers. There are a total of 42 campsites available along Canada Falls and Seboomook Lakes, with a maximum capacity of 12 people per site, except for group sites that can accommodate up to 30 people. Additionally, there are 13 campsites at Lobster Lake, 14 along the Upper West Branch, 22 along Chesuncook Lake, and 29 along the Lower West Branch. Each site is equipped with a fire ring, table, and outhouse. Many of these campsites are accessible only by water. Along the Lower West Branch, there are three large-group sites: Horserace, Salmon Point, and Omaha Beach. Reservations are required for these sites as they are frequently used by rafting groups for lunch. Reservations can be made for one night only, and the site must be vacated by 11 a.m. There are a total of twelve boat launches available for public use. For more information, visit www.maine.gov/dacf/boatlaunches. Picnic areas are also available for visitors to enjoy. The optimal time for paddling in the Seboomook/Penobscot region is typically between May and September. During these months, the fishing conditions are also generally favorable. It is worth noting that the "shoulder season" months, May and September, tend to offer the best fishing opportunities. Recreational dam releases, which enhance the paddling experience, usually occur on Saturdays during July, August, and September. For information regarding the releases at Canada Falls and Seboomook dams, you can contact GLHA at 1-888-323-4341. To inquire about the timing of releases at McKay Station (Ripogenus Dam), you can reach out to Brookfield Power at the same phone number. It's important to be aware that mosquitoes and black flies are most abundant from late May through July, so taking appropriate precautions during this time is advisable. Hunting activities occur during the fall season, with bear baiting typically taking place in September, moose hunting spanning from late September to mid-October, and deer hunting with firearms occurring in November. Snowmobilers can expect favorable trail conditions from December through March. The 20-mile Road to Historic Pittston Farm is plowed in winter; however, it's important to note that most other roads are not consistently plowed, resulting in limited vehicle access during the winter months. For enthusiasts of snowshoeing and backcountry skiing, there are trailheads near Pittston Farm that provide access to the surrounding lands for exploration. Releases of water from the dam on a weekly basis, from July through September, below Canada Falls Lake create a stretch of challenging whitewater spanning 3.5 miles, rated as Class IV to Class V. Between Seboomook Dam and Roll Dam, paddlers can experience Class III whitewater throughout most of the season, with water levels ranging from 350 cubic feet per second (cfs) up to 3,000 cfs or more. Continuing below Roll Dam, the Upper West Branch offers a combination of calm waters and gentle rapids, making it an enjoyable 3- to 4-day trip to Chesuncook Village. Paddlers have the option to conclude their journey at Umbazooksus Stream, covering a distance of 35 miles. Alternatively, they can continue to the eastern end of Chesuncook, adding another 17 miles to their route. For those seeking to explore the Allagash Wilderness Waterway (AWW), they can access it either through Umbazooksus Stream and the Mud Pond Portage or via Caucomgomac Stream and Round Pond. It's important to note that both routes require significant portages. The Lower Penobscot River Corridor features rapids ranging from Class III to Class V, which are recommended to be navigated only by guided whitewater rafts and experienced whitewater paddlers. One of the hiking options in the area is accessing the Appalachian Trail (AT) from Abol Bridge, located off the Golden Road. Baxter State Park manages hiking trails that connect with the AT, offering multiple hiking opportunities in the Abol area. For those paddling on the Upper West Branch, there is an opportunity to take a break from the water and go hiking on Lobster Mountain (2,318 feet). The trailhead can be found at the Jackson Cove campsite on Lobster Lake. The trail, which is clearly marked, spans 2 miles one way and presents a moderately challenging hike. Another popular hiking destination is Big Spencer Mountain (3,230 feet). Although remote, it attracts many hikers. The trail to the flat-topped summit is approximately 2 miles long and includes some ladders and steep sections. To reach the trailhead, take the Greenville Road south toward Kokadjo for about 7 miles from the Golden Road. Look for a rough gravel road called Culvert Road on the right and travel 5 miles until you reach the trailhead on the left. When visiting the Penobscot River Corridor, there are certain considerations to keep in mind: The upper reaches of the Penobscot River Corridor are part of the North Maine Woods recreational system. Visitors must pass through a checkpoint and pay the required day use or camping fees. These fees help cover the costs of managing public access and maintaining recreational facilities. Logging trucks are common in the region, so it's important to watch out for them. Always yield to trucks regardless of their direction since they have the right-of-way. The Maine Department of Inland Fisheries and Wildlife (MDIFW) Warden Service handles search-and-rescue operations and enforces state fish and game laws, boating laws (on inland waters), as well as ATV and snowmobile laws. To learn more about these laws and purchase the necessary licenses, visit www.maine.gov/ifw. Exercise caution with pets: Trappers are permitted to use Maine Public Lands, so it's important to be cautious with your pets to ensure their safety. It is recommended to wear blaze orange clothing during hunting season for increased visibility and safety. Keep in mind that cell phone coverage in these remote areas can be unreliable or non-existent. Do not solely rely on cell phones in case of an emergency. When venturing into these remote areas, plan your trip carefully. Carry a map and compass, inform someone about your intended route and expected return time, monitor weather conditions, and be prepared to wait onshore during windy conditions. River levels below dams can rise rapidly, so exercise caution and respect strong currents. Moose, bears, and other large animals are abundant in the area. Observe them from a safe distance and avoid disturbing or flushing wildlife. When camping, ensure that food items are securely stored to prevent wildlife from being attracted to your campsite. Keep tents free of food and food odors. Only start fires in authorized campsites with fire rings. Do not cut live vegetation for firewood. Burn only locally sourced wood to prevent the spread of forest pests. For more information, visit www.maine.gov/forestpests. In the vicinity of the Penobscot River Corridor, there are several noteworthy destinations within the Maine Highlands Region, particularly in Piscataquis County. These include: Moosehead Lake Shoreline Lands: This area consists of various significant parcels of land along the shoreline of Moosehead Lake. One prominent feature is Mount Kineo, which offers five miles of hiking trails and is well-known among outdoor enthusiasts. Nahmakanta Public Lands: Spanning over 43,000 acres, Nahmakanta Public Lands provide opportunities for lakeside camping and hiking. It boasts 12 miles of exceptionally scenic hiking trails, including a section of the renowned Appalachian Trail. The Allagash Wilderness Waterway is a remarkable stretch of 92 miles that offers breathtaking canoeing and fishing experiences. It is the only river in Maine designated as a "National Scenic and Wild River." Baxter State Park is a vast park spanning over 200,000 acres and encompassing 46 mountain peaks, including the renowned Mt. Katahdin. The park offers abundant opportunities for hiking, boating, and camping, and it serves as the northern terminus of the Appalachian Trail. The Debsconeag Lakes Wilderness Area, managed by The Nature Conservancy, covers an expansive area of 46,271 acres. It features mature forests and boasts the highest concentration of pristine, remote ponds in the New England region.

NOTES:

PASSPORT STAMPS

PASSPORT STAMPS

POPHAM BEACH STATE PARK

COUNTY: SAGADAHOC **ESTABLISHED:** - **AREA (AC/HA):** 605 / 244

DATE VISITED: **LODGING:** **WHO I WENT WITH:**

WEATHER: ☀☐ ☁☐ 🌧☐ ❄☐ ⛅☐ 🌫☐ SPRING ☐ SUMMER ☐ FALL ☐ WINTER ☐

FEE(S): **RATING:** ☆ ☆ ☆ ☆ ☆ **WILL I RETURN?** YES / NO

Popham Beach State Park is the most popular beach within Maine's state park system. It offers various amenities such as bathhouses, freshwater solar rinse-off showers, and charcoal grills. However, it's important to note that the movement of sand, influenced by beach dynamics, has significantly affected Popham Beach, resulting in drastic changes to the shoreline and erosion of the dunes. To support the restoration of the dunes, park staff are asking visitors to stay on designated trails leading to the beach and avoid entering vegetated areas. At low tide, it is possible to walk to Fox Island, but please be cautious of the rapidly rising tides to avoid being strande. Located on the south side of the mouth of the Kennebec River, Popham Beach State Park is a rare geological formation in Maine, featuring a long stretch of sandy beach. While relaxing on Popham's sands, visitors can enjoy views of Fox and Wood islands in the distance, with the Kennebec and Morse rivers bordering each end of the beach. The rolling waves of the Atlantic Ocean attract numerous swimmers and surfers, and beachcombing for seashells is a popular activity for strollers along the shore. Lifeguards are present during the summer months, but it should be noted that Popham Beach has strong surf, undertows, and occasional rip tides. Swimmers are advised to stay within their capabilities and swim near the designated lifeguard area. During the summer, you can call the Popham Beach State Park's Hotline at (207) 389-9125 for the latest tide and parking information. Surfers can also visit www.maineharbors.com. The cultural and social history of Popham is still being uncovered. Excavations of the Popham settlement from 1607 and Fort George continue every summer. The park is open year-round, from 9:00 a.m. until sunset every day, unless stated otherwise at the entrance gate. Fees are collected throughout the year at the entrance booth by park staff or through a self-service station. Shark encounters are increasingly common in Maine and New England. It is important to educate yourself on how to stay safe and informed when visiting coastal beaches. To ensure your safety and protect wildlife, it is crucial to adopt a "Be Shark Smart" approach: Observe and adhere to the instructions, signs, and warning flags provided by lifeguards. Be mindful that sharks often hunt for seals in shallow waters. Stay in close proximity to the shore, where rescuers can easily reach you if needed. Engage in activities like swimming, paddling, kayaking, and surfing in groups, and try to minimize splashing. Avoid areas with seals and large schools of fish, as they may attract sharks. Refrain from entering water that is murky or has low visibility, as it can impede your ability to spot potential dangers. Please note that the use of floating devices, face masks, or snorkels is prohibited at surf beaches. However, scuba diving may be permitted with a valid park-issued permit. If you have any questions, please consult the park staff.

Swimmers have the right-of-way over all other water activities, but it is important to remain vigilant and aware of your surroundings and other recreational activities taking place. It is essential to know what to do if caught in a rip current. Swim parallel to the shore until you are out of the rip's outward pull, and then swim towards the shore. Inexperienced swimmers and children should exercise caution and have experienced swimmers accompany them. Remember that even shallow water can present dangers and strong currents. Swimming to the islands is strongly discouraged due to consistently strong currents. The beach is wheelchair accessible, and a beach wheelchair is available on a first-come, first-served basis, subject to availability. Between April 1 and September 30, pets are not permitted on beaches. However, from October 1 through March 31, pets are allowed on state park beaches as long as they are kept on a leash at all times. Horses are permitted on the beach between October 1 and March 31, but it is necessary to obtain a Horse Beach Permit. Picnic tables and charcoal grills are conveniently situated near the beach, offering scenic views of the water. Stand-up paddleboarding is a favored activity at this location. Exploring the coastline via sea kayaking is a fantastic way to appreciate the surroundings. For those looking to launch their trailerable boats, the nearest site is located on the Kennebec River in Phippsburg. This site features a sturdy 150-foot all-tide ramp. Fishing enthusiasts will enjoy surf casting, with striper being the most commonly caught species.

NOTES:

PASSPORT STAMPS

QUODDY HEAD STATE PARK

COUNTY: WASHINGTON	ESTABLISHED: 1962	AREA (AC/HA): 541 / 218

DATE VISITED:	LODGING:	WHO I WENT WITH:

WEATHER: ☀□ ☁□ ☔□ ❄□ ☔□ ☁□   SPRING □ SUMMER □ FALL □ WINTER □

FEE(S):   **RATING:** ☆ ☆ ☆ ☆ ☆   **WILL I RETURN?** YES / NO

Quoddy Head State Park spans 541 acres on the easternmost peninsula of the United States, providing visitors with opportunities to explore a historic lighthouse, enjoy picnics, and hike along scenic trails extending up to 5 miles. The iconic West Quoddy Head Light, Maine's easternmost lighthouse with its distinctive candy-striped appearance, offers breathtaking views of Quoddy Channel, which separates the U.S. and Canada, and the majestic red cliffs of Grand Manan Island in New Brunswick. Originally commissioned by President Thomas Jefferson, the West Quoddy Head Light was first constructed in 1808. The current tower and house, built in 1858, were manned by lightkeepers until 1988 when the U.S. Coast Guard automated the light. The park is renowned for its exceptional wildlife viewing opportunities. During the summer, visitors may spot humpback, minke, and finback whales in the offshore waters, as well as groups of eider, scoter, and old squaw ducks. Various bird species, including kittiwakes, gannets, black-bellied plovers, ruddy turnstones, and purple sandpipers, can be observed perched on Sail Rock. In spring and fall, hundreds of shorebirds gather near the park's western boundary at Lubec Flats and Carrying Place Cove, which was named after a traditional Native American portage site. Birdwatching remains an activity even in winter, with frequent sightings of sea ducks, murres, razorbills, and bald eagles. A leisurely one-mile round-trip walk leads to a unique coastal plateau bog, also known as a heath, where sub-arctic and arctic plants that are rarely seen south of Canada thrive. The predominant vegetation consists of shrubs, including black crowberry, baked appleberry, and Labrador tea, as well as carnivorous plants like pitcher plants and sundew. Another bog, known as Carrying Place Cove Bog, situated at the park's western boundary, holds the distinction of being a National Natural Landmark. The name Quoddy Head derives from the Passamaquoddy tribe, meaning "fertile and beautiful place." These Native American people, also known as the "People of the Dawn," bestowed this name upon the area. The park features remarkable black cliffs that formed during the Silurian Age approximately 420 million years ago. During this time, volcanic magma emerged from beneath the ocean floor and intruded between existing layers of rock. The magma solidified into a coarse-grained rock called gabbro, which is now visible as the overlying rocks have eroded over time. In 1962, the State of Maine acquired much of the current land for the park by purchasing it from various private landowners. As part of the Maine Lights Program, which involved the transfer of ownership of 28 Maine lighthouses from the Coast Guard to nonprofit organizations or agencies, the West Quoddy Head Light deed temporarily went to the Island Institute and, in 1998, to the Maine Bureau of Parks and Lands. The Bureau currently manages the lighthouse, one of the 63 active lighthouses along

Maine's coastline, with support from the nonprofit organization West Quoddy Light Keepers Association. Initially, the lighthouse used sperm whale oil as fuel, followed by lard oil in the 1860s, and then kerosene around 1880. Eventually, electricity was introduced in the 1890s. The light continues to shine with two white flashes every 15 seconds, visible up to 15-18 miles (24-29 km) out at sea. It utilizes an 1858 third-order Fresnel lens standing at 5.5 feet tall. To enhance visibility in snow and fog, the station was adorned with 15 red and white stripes, added during the reconstruction of the house and tower in 1858 when the original stone tower was replaced by brick. Although the tower is closed to visitors, they can explore the former light keeper's quarters, which are now managed by volunteers from the West Quoddy Light Keepers association. The park is often covered in fog, which occurs when warm and moist air from the mainland meets cold air over the surrounding waters. This fog, along with sea breezes, can create chilly conditions even during the peak of summer, so it is advisable to wear layered clothing for comfort. Due to potentially limited visibility caused by fog, it is recommended to carry a park map when hiking the trails. Please pay attention to park boundary signs and refrain from trespassing on adjacent properties. Exercise caution and closely supervise children, especially near cliffs and water, particularly along the Coastal Trail. The tides in the area can fluctuate more than 20 feet and can change rapidly. Keep in mind that the only wheelchair-accessible restroom facilities are located near the lighthouse, which also complies with ADA standards. The first 0.5 miles of the western section of the Coast Guard Trail is accessible as well. To ensure the safety of your belongings, do not leave valuables unattended in your vehicle while visiting the park. During late spring and summer, be prepared for mosquitoes and black flies. Although deer ticks are not abundant, they can be found in the area, so it is advisable to check yourself daily to prevent Lyme disease and other tick-borne illnesses. For more information, you can visit the Centers for Disease Control and Prevention's website at www.cdc.gov/ticks. To preserve the delicate vegetation of the headland, it is important to stay on designated trails or use the stairs provided to access the shore. Visitors are kindly requested not to pick or remove any plants or disturb the ground cover. Camping is not allowed in this day-use park. For camping locations in State Parks, please visit www.campwithme.com. When picnicking, visitors should follow a carry-in, carry-out approach and take all refuse home for recycling. Consumption of alcoholic beverages is strictly prohibited. Fires are only permitted in designated grills and should be fueled by charcoal only. If you bring pets, they must be leashed, attended to, and under control at all times. When observing wildlife, it is advised not to feed, touch, or disturb them. Maintain a respectful distance and enjoy viewing or photographing them without causing any distress. Hunting is not permitted within 1,000 feet of the lighthouse. Hikers at Quoddy Head State Park have the option to explore five different trails that traverse through forests, wetlands, and provide stunning coastal vistas. Some of the trails near the parking area offer limited wheelchair accessibility. To access the shoreline, there is a stairway located near the picnic area. It is important to exercise caution when near high cliffs and bluffs and be prepared for wet and muddy terrain. The Bog Trail, a 1-mile round-trip hike from the trailhead with a 0.2-mile loop around the bog (rated as easy), features a raised boardwalk and informative signs explaining how the plants in this area adapt to the acidic water and nutrient-poor conditions. It is crucial to stay on the boardwalk to avoid damaging the delicate bog plants. For a more challenging trek with breathtaking ocean views, the Coastal Trail offers a 4-mile round-trip hike (rated as moderate). This trail includes some steep and rocky sections and passes notable landmarks such as Gulliver's Hole, formed by the erosion of a vertical fault in the volcanic gabbro rock, High Ledge, a 150-foot bluff, and Green Point, a large ledge where hikers can reach the beach. The Coast Guard Trail provides easy access to a high cliff overlook that showcases the characteristic beauty of the "Bold Coast." From this vantage point, hikers can enjoy views of Lubec Channel and the town of Lubec. Originally used by the lightkeepers, the trail spans 1 mile and is rated as easy-moderate. The first 0.5 miles of the western section of the Coast Guard Trail is accessible to motorized wheelchairs and can be navigated with assistance for non-motorized chairs. The Inland Trail, a 0.75-mile loop hike rated as easy-moderate, takes walkers through conifer woods adorned with mosses and lichens. The trail gradually ascends to Green Point. For a fairly level wooded path running between the Bog Trail and Coastal Trail, the Thompson Trail offers a 1.25-mile route that is rated as easy. Additionally, visitors can enjoy 1,200 feet of sandy beach at Carrying Place Cove. Quoddy Head State Park is situated in the Downeast-Acadia Region, which includes Hancock and Washington Counties and represents the farthest eastern point of the United States. This region offers various nearby attractions, including: Campobello Island in New Brunswick, Canada, which is home to the historic Roosevelt Campobello International Park and East Quoddy Light. Mowry Beach, a 48-acre preserve owned by the Quoddy Regional Land Trust, featuring a wheelchair-accessible 2,100-foot trail and 1,800 feet of beachfront overlooking Lubec Narrows. Cobscook Bay State Park in Edmunds, which provides an excellent base for exploring the easternmost part of Maine. The park offers numerous waterfront camping sites for visitors to enjoy.

NOTES:

PASSPORT STAMPS

RANGE PONDS STATE PARK

COUNTY: ANDROSCOGGIN	ESTABLISHED: 1965	AREA (AC/HA): 740 / 299

DATE VISITED:	LODGING:	WHO I WENT WITH:

WEATHER: ☼□ ☁□ ☷□ ❄□ ⛆□ ☁□   SPRING ☐ SUMMER ☐ FALL ☐ WINTER ☐

FEE(S):	RATING: ☆ ☆ ☆ ☆ ☆	WILL I RETURN? YES / NO

Located a short distance away from Lewiston and Auburn, two major urban areas in Maine, Range Pond State Park warmly welcomes visitors who want to swim, have picnics, and engage in various activities on its wide sandy beach. The main focus of activities is around the waterfront, which is easily accessible due to the smooth paved path that runs alongside the pond for 1000 feet right next to the beach. Water sports are quite popular in the park, with small boats, canoes, kayaks, and windsurf boards visible on the horizon. There is a public boat launch site located at the end of the beach, but please note that it is only suitable for boats with motors of up to 10 horsepower. Stay informed about the dates when the ice melts on Maine's lakes by visiting www.maine.gov/dacf/iceout. Taking leisurely walks along the park's two-mile-long trails is highly recommended. These trails are easy to navigate as they follow old logging roads and railroad beds. Range Pond State Park provides also such activities as fishing, hunting, cross-country skiing, snowmobiling, and snowshoeing. In addition, the park offers a playground and a group shelter accessible to people with disabilities. The park is open throughout the year, from 9:00 a.m. until sunset every day, unless there are specific notices at the gate stating otherwise. Even during the off-season, visitors can still enjoy the park by parking their vehicles outside the gate without blocking it on the days when it is closed, and entering the park on foot within the same hours. However, please note that the park facilities are closed during the off-season. There is a fee for entry into the park, which is charged year-round either at the entry booth by staff or at a self-service station.

NOTES:

PASSPORT STAMPS

RANGELEY LAKE STATE PARK

COUNTY: FRANKLIN	ESTABLISHED: 1960	AREA (AC/HA): 869 / 351

DATE VISITED:	LODGING:	WHO I WENT WITH:

WEATHER: ☼☐ ☁☐ ❄☐ ✶✶✶☐ ⛅☐ ☔☐   SPRING☐ SUMMER☐ FALL☐ WINTER☐

FEE(S):	RATING: ☆ ☆ ☆ ☆ ☆	WILL I RETURN? YES / NO

Rangeley Lake State Park, located in the heart of Maine's Western Mountains, covers an expansive area of 869 acres. This picturesque park offers a range of activities for visitors to enjoy, including hiking, picnicking, camping, wildlife watching, photography, and winter sports. It also embraces the long-standing traditions of fishing and hunting. The park's main attraction is the impressive Rangeley Lake, boasting nine miles of cool and crystal-clear waters. The lake is renowned for its abundant populations of landlocked salmon and trout, thanks to dedicated catch-and-release practices. Outside the park boundaries, the Rangeley area is a haven for outdoor enthusiasts, particularly those interested in four-wheeling and snowmobiling. There are numerous trails available for these activities, providing ample opportunities for thrilling adventures. The campground at Rangeley Lake State Park features 50 spacious sites, thoughtfully arranged and in close proximity to the lakeshore. From the beach within the park, visitors can enjoy magnificent views of the majestic Saddleback Mountain. The park also offers a designated picnic area, a playground for children, and a convenient trailerable boat launch with finger docks. This facility serves both day visitors and campers, providing easy access to the lake for boating activities. During the 1860s, news of the region's renowned brook trout began to spread, attracting sportsmen who desired to fish in the area. As a result, new camps and guide services emerged, catering to these outdoor enthusiasts. Eventually, luxurious hotels were established to accommodate the affluent vacationers who flocked to the region. To facilitate fishing trips on the lakes, guides developed a sleek and slender rowing vessel, which came to be known as the Rangeley boat. The era of the "rusticators," as these vacationers were called, flourished for almost a century until the 1950s. During this time, the region experienced a significant influx of visitors seeking recreational activities and relaxation. However, by the 1950s, the golden era of the rusticators gradually came to an end. In 1960, more than half of the park's land was generously donated to the state by the Oxford and international paper companies. This donation played a pivotal role in establishing Rangeley Lake State Park as a protected area for future generations to enjoy. The water in the lake tends to be cold, and sudden winds can arise, creating hazardous conditions. For the safety of boaters, it is advised to wear a personal flotation device (PFD) at all times. Additionally, it is essential to inform someone about your intended boating route and expected time of return. It is also crucial to carefully monitor the weather and water conditions while on the lake. All motorized boats that are operated on Maine's inland waters are required to purchase and display a Lake and River Protection Sticker. The funds generated from these stickers contribute to the efforts aimed at preventing and monitoring the spread of aquatic invasive species. Individuals who plan to engage in fishing activities, including residents aged 16 and above and non-residents aged 12 and above, must possess a valid fishing license. It is necessary to familiarize oneself with the open water fishing regulations set by the State. These regulations can be found on the website www.maine.gov/ifw/aboutus/laws_rules/index.html. It is important to be prepared for the presence of black flies and mosquitoes, particularly during the months of May and June. Take precautions such as using insect repellent and wearing protective clothing. Additionally, it is advisable to regularly check for deer ticks on your body to prevent the transmission of Lyme disease. There are two main trails in the park: The Moose Corridor Trail: This forested hiking trail spans a distance of 0.7 miles, starting from the park entrance and leading to the ranger station. It offers a scenic route through the woods, allowing visitors to immerse themselves in the natural surroundings. The Lake Trail: This forested trail stretches for 0.9 miles and meanders near the lake. Beginning from the beach path, it heads southward towards the boat launch located at South Cove. On the northern end, the trail concludes at the campground loop road. The Park operates and is staffed from May 15th to October 1st. During the season, the park's day use hours are from 9 a.m. until sunset, unless there are specific signs posted at the gate indicating otherwise. It is highly recommended to make advance reservations for camping. To do so, you can contact the State Park Reservations Office. If you are calling from within Maine, the number to dial is 800-332-1501. If you are calling from outside of Maine, please dial 207-624-9950. Anglers and hunters must adhere to all state hunting laws. Visit www.maine.gov/ifw/ for more information. Hunting is prohibited between June 1st and Labor Day. Firearms should not be discharged within 300 feet of picnic areas, camping areas, parking areas, marked hiking trails, or other developed areas. Loaded firearms are not permitted at campsites or on hiking trails. Rangeley Lake State Park is situated in the Lakes and Mountains Region of Maine, specifically within Franklin and Oxford Counties. This region represents the westernmost part of the state and is renowned for its natural beauty. In close proximity to the park, there are several points of interest that visitors can explore: Mt. Blue State Park/Tumbledown Public Lands: This park attracts visitors with its camping facilities, opportunities for swimming in Webb Lake, hiking trails, mountain biking routes, as well as areas designated for ATV riding and horseback riding. Grafton Notch State Park/Mahoosucs Public Lands: This park offers a range of activities including hiking, picnicking, and sightseeing. Within its expansive 35,000-acre area, visitors can discover numerous waterfalls, gorges, and stunning mountainous landscapes. Height of Land: Located on Route 17, this famous overlook provides an awe-inspiring view of the surrounding region. Visitors can enjoy a panoramic vista that captures the beauty of the area. Bald Mountain: Situated nearby, Bald Mountain offers a scenic 2-mile roundtrip hike with diverse terrain. At the summit, hikers are rewarded with an open vista and a 360-degree view of the surrounding landscape from an observation deck located on a converted Forest Service fire tower. Coos Canyon: This picturesque gorge is located along the Swift River in Byron. Visitors have the opportunity to engage in activities such as gold panning and swimming while enjoying the natural beauty of the area.

NOTES:

PASSPORT STAMPS

REID STATE PARK

COUNTY: SAGADAHOC	ESTABLISHED: 1950	AREA (AC/HA): 770 / 311
DATE VISITED:	LODGING:	WHO I WENT WITH:

WEATHER: ☀☐ ☁☐ ☷☐ ❄☐ ⛈☐ ☔☐   SPRING ☐ SUMMER ☐ FALL ☐ WINTER ☐

| FEE(S): | RATING: ☆ ☆ ☆ ☆ ☆ | WILL I RETURN? YES / NO |

Reid State Park holds the esteemed distinction of being Maine's first State-owned Saltwater Beach. In 1946, Walter E. Reid, a prosperous businessman and resident of Georgetown, generously donated land to the State of Maine with the intention of preserving it for eternity. A few years later, Reid State Park came into existence. Today, the park attracts thousands of visitors who delight in its expansive sandy beaches, such as Mile and Half Mile, which are a rarity in Maine. These beaches serve not only as recreational havens but also as crucial nesting grounds for endangered species like least terns and piping plovers. They also provide resting and feeding areas for other shorebirds. One of the park's exceptional features is its large sand dunes, a geological marvel not commonly found along Maine's coastline. In May 2015, Reid State Park beach was named the number one surfing spot in New England by Boston Globe magazine. From the vantage point of Griffith Head, a rocky headland that overlooks the park, visitors are treated to breathtaking ocean views and can catch sight of lighthouses situated on Seguin Island, The Cuckolds, and Hendricks Head. Several islands are also visible, including Damariscove, which was once a thriving fishing community during Colonial times; Outer Head, a protected sanctuary for terns; and Southport, where renowned naturalist Rachel Carson penned her influential book, Silent Spring. The Little River Trail offers a Natural Heritage Hike experience. These hikes provide narratives that guide hikers through the diverse ecological, geological, and cultural aspects encountered along 25 of Maine's most popular hiking trails. They offer hikers a deeper understanding of the natural environments they traverse.

NOTES:

PASSPORT STAMPS

ROQUE BLUFFS STATE PARK

COUNTY: WASHINGTON	ESTABLISHED: 1969	AREA (AC/HA): 274 / 110

DATE VISITED: **LODGING:** **WHO I WENT WITH:**

WEATHER: ☀☐ ⛅☐ 🌧☐ ❄☐ ⛈☐ 🌫☐   SPRING ☐ SUMMER ☐ FALL ☐ WINTER ☐

FEE(S): **RATING:** ☆ ☆ ☆ ☆ ☆   **WILL I RETURN?** YES / NO

Roque Bluffs State Park, situated on Schoppee Point south of Machias, offers visitors a diverse range of coastal landscapes to explore within its 274 acres. The park boasts a stunning half-mile crescent-shaped beach comprised of sand and pebbles along Englishman Bay. This picturesque shoreline is complemented by the shallow waters of Simpson Pond, a 60-acre body of water, which provides the opportunity for invigorating saltwater swims and warmer freshwater soaks. Between the beach and the pond, several picnic areas and a children's play area can be found near the parking area. A network of trails spans three miles inland from the shore, leading visitors through old orchards, fields, and woods, with paths that trace the rocky edges of Great Cove and Pond Cove. The diverse habitats found at Roque Bluffs State Park support a rich abundance of wildlife, making it a haven for birdwatchers throughout the year. Bald eagles can be observed in the area year-round, and various migratory bird species make stopovers during the spring and fall seasons. Birdwatchers may have the opportunity to spot less common waterfowl, including Barrow's Goldeneye, Redhead and Gadwall ducks, and Hooded Mergansers. During the summer months, beachgoers can also observe sandpipers, plovers, and interesting gull species such as the ring-billed gull. Both Englishman Bay and Simpson Pond offer opportunities for exploration by canoe or kayak, with rental kayaks available specifically for use on Simpson Pond. Anglers can enjoy fishing in the pond, which is stocked with brook trout in the spring and brown trout throughout much of the summer. Bait fishermen also utilize the pond during the fall and winter seasons. The sandy and pebbled beach found at Roque Bluffs State Park offers a unique geological feature along the Downeast coast, which is predominantly characterized by rugged cliffs and cobble shores. This beach was formed by the accumulation of sediment that eroded from a prominent glacial moraine located to the east. At the eastern end of the beach, there is a bedrock outcrop where visitors can observe glacial striations—deep grooves etched into the bedrock as a result of the glacier's movement toward the southeast. The presence of these glacial remnants has earned Roque Bluffs State Park the distinction of being Stop #29 on Maine's Ice Age Trail, which provides further information about the state's glacial history (for more details, visit http://iceagetrail.umaine.edu/). Roque Bluffs beach is one of the five State Park beaches within the 32-unit Maine Coastal Barrier System. These beaches serve as protective buffers along the coast, shielding it from storms and offering valuable habitat for plants and wildlife. Offshore, visitors can catch sight of Libby Lighthouse, formerly known as Machias Lighthouse, as it marks the entrance to Machias Bay. This historic lighthouse, constructed in 1817, remains an active beacon to this day. The park offers handicap-accessible parking areas located at the trailhead, beach, and boat launch. Additionally, there are handicap-accessible privies available at the beach parking lots, although they do not have running water. Visitors can make use of the picnic area, which includes tables and grills, and some of them are also handicap-accessible. There are playgrounds available for recreational activities. Please note that there are no reservable group areas, but you can contact the park for assistance in planning a special event. For those interested in boating, there is a trailerable boat launch situated at the end of Schoppee Point. The main trailhead parking lot is located a quarter-mile east of the beach parking lots, up the hill towards Roque Bluffs village. Another access point to the trail network is available from the beach parking area through Starr Trail. There are three primary hiking trails: Houghton's Hill Trail, Mihill Trail, and Pond Cove Trail, as well as a few smaller connector trails like Blueberry Camp Trail and Larry's Loop. These trails offer a variety of hiking options, taking you through fields and woodlands that border Pond and Great coves. Each trail is marked with a specific color code and clear markers on the ground for easy navigation. Houghton's Hill Trail (0.8 mile, marked with red blazes) provides a pleasant walk through the woods from the main trailhead to Pond Cove. Along the trail, there is a picnic table situated halfway, offering a spot to rest or enjoy a snack. Mihill Trail (1 mile, marked with yellow blazes) can be accessed via Houghton's Hill Trail or the Starr Trail leading to Houghton's Hill Trail. This trail takes you up a small hill and runs along the shore of Great Cove, leading to the northern end of the Pond Cove Trail. Look for two turnoffs along the way that offer shortcuts back to Houghton's Hill, creating what is known as Larry's Loop. Pond Cove Trail (0.8 mile, marked with green blazes) guides you through meadows and woods on mostly flat terrain, offering picturesque views over Pond Cove. Blueberry Camp Trail (0.2 mile, marked with blue blazes) provides an alternative route to Houghton's Hill Trail, featuring a small hill climb. Starr Trail (0.3 mile) skirts a wetland area and serves as a connection from the beach area to the trail network, allowing for easy access between the two. Please ensure that you visit Roque Bluffs State Park during daylight hours, as the main area is gated at night and access is restricted. It is advisable to bring your own potable water, as there is no water available on-site. Remember not to leave your valuables unattended in your vehicle to prevent theft or loss. While swimming is allowed in both Englishman's Bay and Simpson Pond, please be aware that there are no lifeguards on duty. If you plan to fish off the beach in Englishman's Bay, exercise caution around nearby swimmers. Kayakers have the option to launch their boats from the beach in Englishman's Bay. However, please note that the State does not own any nearby islands, so public access to those areas is not guaranteed. It is important to be an experienced kayaker if you decide to paddle in the open waters of Englishman's Bay due to potential weather conditions such as fog and wind. Remember to wear a life vest or personal flotation device (PFD) for safety. Anglers and hunters visiting the area are required to adhere to all State hunting laws, which can be found at www.maine.gov/ifw/. It's important to note that hunting is not allowed between June 1st and Labor Day. Additionally, the discharge of weapons is strictly prohibited within 300 feet of any picnic area, camping area, parking area, marked hiking trail, or other developed areas. For the safety of all visitors, loaded firearms are not permitted at campsites or on hiking trails. The park is accessible to visitors from May 15th to October 1st, specifically for day-use activities. During this time, the park is open from 9 a.m. until sunset, unless there are specific instructions indicated at the gate. Although the parking areas are closed and gated for the rest of the year, visitors are still welcome to explore the trails and enjoy the beach throughout all seasons. Roque Bluffs State Park is situated in the Downeast-Acadia Region, which encompasses Hancock and Washington Counties and represents the easternmost part of the United States. This region offers various attractions and destinations for visitors to explore: Cobscook Bay State Park provides waterfront campsites and serves as a great starting point for exploring the easternmost part of Maine. Cutler Coast Public Lands offer 10 miles of trails along the stunning and dramatic "bold coast," with 4.5 miles of coastline. Fort O'Brien State Historic Site played a significant role in guarding the Machias River during the American Revolution, War of 1812, and Civil War. Quoddy Head State Park features a picturesque lighthouse and scenic waterfront trails, located at the easternmost point of land in the United States. Rocky Lake Public Lands cover 10,000 acres of land, ideal for activities like canoeing, fishing, and backcountry camping.

NOTES:

PASSPORT STAMPS

SCARBOROUGH BEACH STATE PARK

COUNTY: CUMBERLAND   **ESTABLISHED:** -   **AREA (AC/HA):** - / -

DATE VISITED: **LODGING:**   **WHO I WENT WITH:**

WEATHER: ☀☐ ☁☐ ☔☐ ❄☐ ⛈☐ 🌫☐   SPRING ☐ SUMMER ☐ FALL ☐ WINTER ☐

FEE(S):   **RATING:** ☆ ☆ ☆ ☆ ☆   **WILL I RETURN?** YES / NO

Scarborough Beach offers excellent swimming opportunities in New England, with water temperatures reaching the high 60s Fahrenheit throughout July and August. Currents are a daily occurrence, so swimming in a designated lifeguard zone is strongly recommended. As for parking, there are a total of 285 spaces available on-site and an additional 125 spaces off-site. On weekends, the on-site parking spaces typically reach capacity by 11:30 am, and the off-site spaces by 12:30 pm. It is recommended to arrive early if you plan to visit on weekends. Hunting is prohibited from May 1 to September 30. Trapping is only allowed if it adheres to the laws of the State of Maine, the Maine Department of Inland Fisheries and Wildlife, and the Town of Scarborough Ordinances. Prior written consent must be obtained from the Bureau of Parks and Lands.

NOTES:

PASSPORT STAMPS

SEBAGO LAKE STATE PARK

COUNTY: CUMBERLAND	ESTABLISHED: 1938	AREA (AC/HA): 1,400 / 566
DATE VISITED:	LODGING:	WHO I WENT WITH:

WEATHER: ☀☐ ☁☐ ☷☐ ❄☐ ⚡☐ ☔☐   SPRING ☐ SUMMER ☐ FALL ☐ WINTER ☐

FEE(S):   RATING: ☆ ☆ ☆ ☆ ☆   WILL I RETURN? YES / NO

Sebago Lake State Park is open year-round, from 9:00 a.m. until sunset every day, unless otherwise indicated at the entrance gate. A fee is collected throughout the year either by the park staff at the entry booth or through a self-service station. The park was established in 1938 as one of the original five state parks in Maine. Nestled along the shore of the state's deepest and second largest lake, this forested park offers year-round recreational activities for numerous visitors. Located near the foothills of the White Mountains, the park spans 1,400 acres and features sandy beaches, expansive woodlands, ponds, bogs, a river, and diverse habitats that support a wide range of plant and animal species. During the summer months, visitors can enjoy activities such as swimming, sport fishing, camping, and boating. The park's campground, consisting of 250 sites, is a popular destination for families seeking memorable vacations that create lasting memories year after year. The wooded areas provide a pleasant retreat from the sun and beach activities. Whether hiking on marked trails or cycling along park roads, visitors have various ways to appreciate the natural beauty of the park. Additionally, the park operates the historic Songo Lock. Sebago Lake, which was sculpted by ancient rivers and shaped by glaciers during the Ice Age, fills a basin composed of weathered granite that has endured for millions of years. Thanks to these glacial formations, present-day visitors can partake in a wide range of water sports on the expansive 45-square-mile lake. For those interested in exploring the park's geological features in-depth, guided tours are available through "The Geology of Sebago Lake State Park" program. The park provides a campground area where visitors can set up their tents or park their RVs. RV campsites are equipped with electric and water hookups, enabling campers to conveniently access these essential amenities. Shower facilities are provided for campers and visitors. For RV campers, a dedicated dumping station is available. There is a food service available within the park, allowing visitors to purchase meals, snacks, and beverages during their visit. A designated sheltered area is provided for group picnics, offering a convenient space for gatherings and enjoying meals together. The park features a playground area designed for children. Sebago Lake State Park offers a designated boat launch area suitable for trailered boats. For those interested in fishing during the summer, the park's boat launch provides convenient access to the lake. The trails at Sebago Lake State Park are well-marked and offer an enjoyable experience for hikers of all skill levels. These trails, ranging from easy to moderate difficulty, wind their way through various forest types and woodland areas, providing glimpses of the Songo River and segments of the north shore of Sebago Lake. While exploring the trails, it is common to come across wildlife such as deer and bald eagles. During the winter season, trail maps specifically designed for cross-country skiing and snowshoeing can be obtained at the parking areas. These trails are repurposed as hiking trails during the summer months. Winter camping is an option available within the park, and visitors can also enjoy ice fishing in designated areas. It is important to note that Sebago Lake often takes longer to freeze compared to other local lakes and ponds, so caution is essential before venturing onto the ice. It is advised to test the ice thickness regularly, ensuring it is safe and adequate. For cross-country skiing enthusiasts, Sebago Lake State Park offers a total of 5.5 miles of groomed trails on the Casco side. Among these, 3.7 miles have set tracks for classic skiing, while 1.5 miles are specifically groomed for skate skiing. On the Naples side of the park, there are 6 miles of ungroomed trails available. These trails cater to skiers of varying skill levels, ranging from easy to moderate difficulty. They meander through diverse forest types and woodland areas, providing scenic views along the Songo River and a section of the north shore of Sebago Lake.

NOTES:

PASSPORT STAMPS

SHACKFORD HEAD STATE PARK

COUNTY: WASHINGTON	ESTABLISHED: 1989	AREA (AC/HA): 90 / 36

DATE VISITED:	LODGING:	WHO I WENT WITH:

WEATHER: ☀□ ☁□ ♨□ ❄□ ☔□ ☁□   SPRING ☐ SUMMER ☐ FALL ☐ WINTER ☐

FEE(S):	RATING: ☆ ☆ ☆ ☆ ☆	WILL I RETURN? YES / NO

Shackford Head State Park is located near downtown Eastport, which is the easternmost city in the United States. The park spans 90 acres on Moose Island and offers scenic views of Cobscook Bay. This peninsula, situated at the entrance of Cobscook Bay, surrounds the western side of Broad Cove. The headland is traversed by several miles of trails. Starting from the parking area, a hiking trail leads through wooded areas to a rocky headland that stands 173 feet above sea level. Along the way, there are several small beaches and protected coves. From this vantage point, visitors can observe Campobello Island in New Brunswick, Canada, the town of Lubec, and the Eastport cargo pier on Estes Head. Additionally, there are aquaculture pens where Atlantic salmon are bred. The park's trails provide excellent opportunities for wildlife observation. In the woodland areas, visitors can spot warblers and hermit thrushes, while along the shoreline, bald eagles, common terns, and spotted sandpipers can be seen. Ornithologists have identified 28 different bird species that nest on the headland. Shackford Head received its name from one of the early settlers of the town, Captain John Shackford. He was a soldier in the Revolutionary War and arrived in Eastport with his family around 1783. Captain Shackford, who was born and raised in Massachusetts, spent the majority of his 87 years residing in Eastport. He owned the headland and utilized Broad Cove as an anchorage for his ship. He passed away on December 25, 1840, and was laid to rest next to his wife in the nearby Hillside East Cemetery. In the early 1900s, Cony Beach on Shackford Head became the site where five ships that had served in the Civil War, namely the U.S.S. Franklin, U.S.S. Minnesota, U.S.S. Richmond, U.S.S. Vermont, and U.S.S. Wabash, were intentionally burned for salvaging purposes, specifically to recover brass and iron. A memorial plaque on the site provides additional information about this particular chapter in the history of the headland. During the 1970s, there was a proposal by the Pittston Company to construct an oil refinery at Shackford Head. However, this plan faced strong opposition due to the navigational risks present in Cobscook Bay and the exceptional value of the area's wildlife. When the property went up for sale in 1988, the Eastport Land Trust sought assistance from the State's Land for Maine's Future (LMF) Program to ensure that the land remained in its natural state for public enjoyment. The LMF Program played a role in funding the acquisition of the land in 1989, and it is now owned and managed by the Maine Department of Conservation. The park is often covered in fog, which occurs when warm and moist air from the mainland meets cold air over the surrounding waters. This fog, combined with sea breezes, can create chilly conditions, even during the peak of summer. It is advisable to bring extra layers of clothing to stay warm. Due to the fog, visibility can be low, so it is recommended to carry a park map when hiking trails. When walking on cliffside trails or near the shore, exercise caution and keep a close eye on children. The tides in the area can fluctuate by more than 20 feet and can come in quickly, posing potential risks. Respect the park boundaries and do not trespass on adjacent properties, as indicated by boundary signs. It is essential to bring your own drinking water for hikes and picnics, as there is no water available within the park. During late spring and summer, be prepared for the presence of mosquitoes and black flies. While not abundant, deer ticks can also be found in the area. It is advisable to check yourself daily to prevent Lyme disease. The park is open every day from 9 a.m. until sunset, starting from May 15th through October 15th. During the off-season, visitors are welcome during daylight hours, but they should exercise caution in snowy or icy conditions. The trail system at Shackford Head State Park consists of both easy walking trails and more challenging, uneven terrain. Some trails near the parking area offer wheelchair accessibility, but the entire trail network is not accessible. While enjoying the scenic overlooks, it is important to be cautious near high cliffs and bluffs. For the best access to the shore, Cony Beach (near the parking area) or the Broad Cove Trail are recommended. The Shackford Head Overlook, a 1.2-mile roundtrip trail, offers excellent views of Cobscook Bay and the surrounding area. If you prefer more challenging terrain, you can extend your hike by adding the Ship Point Trail, which is an additional half-mile loop. To complete a total distance of approximately 2 miles, return to the parking lot via the Schooner Trail. Please note that certain trails may be temporarily closed when eagles are nesting on park lands. These closures are in place to protect the young eagle families from disturbance. It is important to respect the signs indicating trail closures. There are several park rules that must be strictly followed, including: The use of intoxicating beverages is strictly prohibited. Hunting, camping, and the use of motorized vehicles are not allowed. Wildlife should not be fed, touched, or disturbed. Pets must be kept on a leash at all times, with a leash length of less than 4 feet. All trash must be carried out of the park. While swimming is permitted on other beaches at Shackford Head, it is not recommended at Cony Beach, located just east of the parking area, as it was the site where the Civil War ships were demolished. Shackford Head State Park is located within the Downeast-Acadia Region, which comprises Hancock and Washington Counties and represents the easternmost corner of the United States. There are several nearby destinations worth visiting, including: Campobello Island in New Brunswick, which is home to the historic Roosevelt Campobello International Park and East Quoddy Light. Cobscook Bay State Park in Edmunds, which serves as a great base for exploring the easternmost part of Maine and offers numerous waterfront camping sites. Mowry Beach, a 48-acre preserve owned by the Quoddy Regional Land Trust, featuring a wheelchair-accessible 2,100-foot trail and 1,800 feet of beachfront overlooking Lubec Narrows. Quoddy Head State Park in Lubec, offering 5 miles of picturesque cliffside and wooded trails, a rocky beach along the Bold Coast, and a lighthouse situated at the tip of America's easternmost peninsula.

NOTES:

PASSPORT STAMPS

SWAN LAKE STATE PARK

COUNTY: WALDO   ESTABLISHED: -   AREA (AC/HA): 67 / 27

DATE VISITED: LODGING: WHO I WENT WITH:

WEATHER: ☀☐ ☁☐ ☔☐ ❄☐ ⛅☐ 🌫☐   SPRING ☐ SUMMER ☐ FALL ☐ WINTER ☐

FEE(S):   RATING: ☆ ☆ ☆ ☆ ☆   WILL I RETURN?   YES / NO

The park is situated on the picturesque Swan Lake and offers various amenities for visitors. Visitors to the park can engage in various activities, including canoeing, fishing, hunting, and swimming. There is a designated swimming area with lifeguards on duty, picnic sites equipped with grills, and walking trails for leisurely strolls. Toilets and changing facilities are also available for use. For larger gatherings, there is a private group shelter available for reservation, which incurs a fee. Reservations for the group shelter can be made starting from the first working day of January for the same year. The shelter is equipped with volleyball and horseshoe facilities, along with a handicapped-accessible toilet. Swan Lake State Park is open daily from 9:00 a.m. until sunset during the period from Memorial Day to Labor Day. A fee is charged for entry, and only cash or check payments are accepted; credit cards are not accepted. However, visitors can still enjoy the park during the off-season by parking outside the gate, ensuring it is not blocked, and walking in during the same hours. Admission fees should be placed in the self-service collection canister. It's important to note that facilities

NOTES:

PASSPORT STAMPS

SWANS FALLS CAMPGROUND

COUNTY: OXFORD	ESTABLISHED: -	AREA (AC/HA): - / -

DATE VISITED:	LODGING:	WHO I WENT WITH:

WEATHER: ☼☐ ☁☐ ☂☐ ❄☐ ⛆☐ 〰☐   SPRING ☐ SUMMER ☐ FALL ☐ WINTER ☐

FEE(S):   **RATING:** ☆ ☆ ☆ ☆ ☆   **WILL I RETURN?** YES / NO

Swan's Falls Campground provides 18 tent sites nestled within a pine forest along the scenic Saco River. Visitors can enjoy access to fantastic opportunities for day trips or extended adventures by canoe or kayak. The campground is situated in the Mt. Washington Valley, offering convenient proximity to the White Mountain National Forest. The park is overseen by the Saco River Recreational Council (SRRC) through an agreement with the Maine Department of Agriculture, Conservation, and Forestry. The campground offers various amenities, including outhouses for restroom facilities, fire rings for campfires, water spigots for convenient access to water, and picnic tables for outdoor dining and relaxation. Additionally, two specific sites, namely sites 11 and 20, feature a lean-to structure for added shelter. The park offers convenient amenities, including a camp store and visitor center, designated areas for day and overnight parking, as well as a small campground managed by the SRRC. The park is located right in the heart of Fryeburg, and it only takes a 15-minute drive to reach North Conway, New Hampshire. Transporting firewood can introduce harmful exotic insects and diseases that can severely damage forests. To protect forests, it is strongly advised not to transport firewood. Instead, it is recommended to purchase firewood from a local source to minimize the risk of spreading pests and diseases.

NOTes:

PASSPORT STAMPS

TWO LIGHTS STATE PARK

COUNTY: CUMBERLAND	ESTABLISHED: 1961	AREA (AC/HA): 41 / 16

DATE VISITED:　　**LODGING:**　　**WHO I WENT WITH:**

WEATHER: ☀☐ ☁☐ ☔☐ ❄☐ ⛅☐ 🌊☐　　SPRING ☐ SUMMER ☐ FALL ☐ WINTER ☐

FEE(S):　　**RATING:** ☆ ☆ ☆ ☆ ☆　　**WILL I RETURN?** YES / NO

The park is open throughout the year from 9:00 a.m. until sunset, unless there are specific notices at the entrance. There is an admission fee. Two Lights State Park is a well-liked destination for both residents of Maine and visitors who appreciate the state's famous rocky coastline. Established in 1961, the park spans 41 acres of rocky cliffs. From its elevated position above the rugged coast and rolling waves, visitors can enjoy expansive views of Casco Bay and the vast Atlantic Ocean. The park got its name from the two adjacent lighthouses located just outside the park, at the end of Two Lights Road. These lighthouses were built in 1828 and were the first pair of twin lighthouses on Maine's coastline. While the eastern lighthouse is still operational and can be seen from 17 miles at sea, it is not open to the public. The western lighthouse ceased functioning in 1924 and has since been converted into a private residence. One of these lighthouses was famously depicted in Edward Hopper's renowned painting titled "Lighthouse at Two Lights." Before it became a park, the area was used as a coastal defense installation during World War II. Some remnants of this military use can still be seen today, such as an observation tower and several bunkers within the park. Visitors can enjoy picnics at the tables located on the hills facing the ocean, providing them with breathtaking views while indulging in a barbecue or clambake during the afternoon. The park also offers a shelter and group sites that can be reserved for a fee. Additionally, there is a playground for children and an ice skating pond, which remains open year-round. Those who prefer walking or hiking can relish the refreshing sea breezes along the shoreline trails and witness ships sailing into and out of Portland Harbor. It's important to keep in mind that ocean breezes can cool down summer afternoons, so it's advisable to bring warm clothing for a pleasant visit. Additionally, when walking along the rocky area near the ocean, it is recommended to stay at least 20 feet away from the surf and keep a close watch on children under your care. Crescent Beach State Park and Kettle Cove State Park are conveniently located just half a mile away from Two Lights State Park.

NOTES:

PASSPORT STAMPS

VAUGHAN WOODS MEMORIAL STATE PARK

COUNTY: YORK		ESTABLISHED: 1949	AREA (AC/HA): 165 / 66
DATE VISITED:	LODGING:	WHO I WENT WITH:	
WEATHER: ☀☁️❄️❄️⛈️🌫️		SPRING ☐ SUMMER ☐ FALL ☐ WINTER ☐	
FEE(S):	RATING: ☆☆☆☆☆	WILL I RETURN? YES / NO	

The park is open from 9:00 a.m. until sunset every day between Memorial Day and Labor Day, unless there are specific notices at the gate. There is an admission fee, and only cash or check payments are accepted. Visitors can still enjoy the park during the off-season by parking outside the gate without blocking it and entering on foot during the same hours. Please remember to place the admission fee in the self-service collection canister. It's important to note that facilities are closed during the off-season. Vaughan Woods Memorial State Park is a sprawling 165-acre forested area located along the picturesque Salmon Falls River. Within the park, there are picnic facilities available, as well as hiking trails that meander through ancient stands of pine and hemlock trees. The trails are interconnected, forming a single extensive loop that spans over 3 miles. Visitors can opt to walk shorter sections of the loop if they prefer. While exploring the trails within this forest, you will encounter diverse and intriguing terrain: The Bridle Path, spanning 0.7 miles, traverses gently rolling high ground, as does the Bridle Path Loop, which covers 0.3 miles. However, as you venture further, the land abruptly descends over 150 feet towards the river, where streams have carved deep valleys. The Scenic River Run, extending for 0.8 miles, takes you along the riverbanks and through these picturesque stream valleys, particularly near the Trail's End. Warren Way, named after James Warren, who once owned and resided on this land, guides you through the trails. Follow the Bridle Path southward from this trail to discover a plaque commemorating the former location of the Warren homestead and house. The place names in this area reveal the rich history and connection to the land. As you approach the park along Oldfields Road, you enter an area known as "oldfields" since the colonial times. Native Americans in this region utilized controlled fires to manage wildlife habitats and clear land for cultivating crops such as corn, beans, and squash. After the soil lost its fertility after 8-10 years, they would move on to a new area for farming while allowing the previous land to grow into berry bushes, brush, and eventually transform into a forest. This practice ensured that farming, berrying, and hunting areas remained in close proximity. Around 1785, Jonathan Hamilton, a merchant, constructed the Hamilton House at a location offering a magnificent view of the river and the surrounding countryside. During the early 1800s, the landscape visible from this vantage point consisted of small fields used for growing hay, pastures, and row crops. At that time, only 3% of the land that would later become Vaughan Woods was covered in forest. However, by 1898, when Emily Tyson, a wealthy resident of Boston, purchased the Hamilton House and its property, no open farmland remained. Instead, the area consisted of brushlands, young white pines that grew from old pastures, and a small forest containing pine, hemlock, and hardwood trees. Mrs. Tyson and her daughter, Elizabeth Vaughan, held deep respect for nature and diligently managed the forest to promote its health and preserve its beauty. They also restored the Hamilton House, which is now open to the public during specific seasons and is owned and managed by Historic New England. In 1949, Elizabeth Vaughan generously bequeathed her beautiful forest to the State of Maine, with the stipulation that it be maintained "in its natural wild state" as the Vaughan Woods Memorial. Elizabeth Vaughan, a lover of nature and an accomplished horsewoman, delighted in daily rides and walks through this forest. Nearby attractions in the area include: Fort McClary State Historic Site: For over 275 years, a fort has stood as a protective stronghold at the southern gateway to Kittery, Maine, guarding the approaches to the Piscataqua River. The current fort, Fort McClary, is named after Major Andrew McClary, a New Hampshire native who lost his life at the Battle of Bunker Hill during the Revolutionary War. Ferry Beach State Park: Situated off Route 9 on Bay View Road, between Old Orchard Beach and Camp Ellis in Saco, this park offers a magnificent view of miles of pristine white sand beaches stretching between the Saco River and Pine Point. In addition to beach activities, forested trails provide a serene escape from the sun, giving visitors the opportunity to encounter a rare stand of tupelo (black gum) trees at this latitude. Amenities such as changing rooms, picnic areas, nature trails, and guided nature programs are available for visitors to enjoy. Hamilton House and Gardens: An historic house and its meticulously maintained gardens, formerly the residence of Colonel Jonathan Hamilton, who constructed the house in 1787 overlooking the Salmon Falls River. In 1898, Mrs. Tyson-Vaughan acquired the property, transforming it into a gathering place for intellectuals from Boston. A portion of the property, now known as Vaughan Woods, was generously donated by Mrs. Tyson Vaughan as a natural preserve to the State of Maine in honor of her late husband. The setting of Sarah Orne Jewett's novel, "The Tory Lover," draws inspiration from the Hamilton House. John Paul Jones State Historic Site: Situated in Kittery on US Route 1, just before the bridge to Badger's Island, this site is named after John Paul Jones, a renowned naval commander during the American Revolutionary War. Jones is famous for his leadership aboard the Ranger, the only ship ever to be saluted by a foreign power. The John Paul Jones State Historic Site is also home to the Maine Sailors' and Soldiers' Memorial, a sculpted stone artwork created by Bashka Paeff, paying tribute to the brave men and women who served in the military.

NOTES:

PASSPORT STAMPS

WARREN ISLAND STATE PARK

COUNTY: WALDO   **ESTABLISHED:** 1959   **AREA (AC/HA):** 70 / 28

DATE VISITED: **LODGING:**   **WHO I WENT WITH:**

WEATHER: ☀□ ☁□ ⛅□ ❄□ ⛈□ 🌫□   SPRING □ SUMMER □ FALL □ WINTER □

FEE(S):   **RATING:** ☆ ☆ ☆ ☆ ☆   **WILL I RETURN?** YES / NO

Warren Island State Park was gifted to the people of Maine by the Town of Islesboro in 1959. This 70-acre island, located around three miles off the coast of Lincolnville, became Maine's first State Park specifically developed for boating enthusiasts. Historical British Admiralty charts indicate the presence of a single dwelling, believed to be owned by Nathaniel Pendleton, in the center of the island before the American Revolutionary War. During the nineteenth century, at least six families resided on Warren Island. The Warren family, headed by George Warren and his wife Lydia Hatch, lived there for nearly sixty years. They occupied a sturdy farmhouse surrounded by cleared farmland near the center of the island. George Warren's son, Capt. J.W. Warren, lived on the northwest shore, opposite Seven Hundred Acre Island. A.J. Williams owned land on the northeast end of the island, where David Williams is believed to have lived. In 1861, George Warren sold the island to Mansfield Clark of Islesboro for $600. One acre was reserved by George Warren and owned by David Williams. David Williams, married to Mrs. Samuel Haskell, resided halfway along the northeast shore. The foundation rock of their former residence can still be found at what is now Picnic Site #1. Three other families, Joseph F. McKinney, Elijah Dyer, and Jeremiah Warren, were known to have lived on the island in the late 1800s. A gravestone marked "Mrs. Zilica, wife of Isaac Thomas; died July 9, 1841, age 22 years" is located off the southeast section of the trail leading from the middle of the island to camping site #7. It is unclear whether the Thomas family actually lived on Warren Island or if they resided on Seven Hundred Acre Island and were buried on Warren Island. In 1899, Warren Island was sold to Wm. H. Folwell, who built what is believed to be the most expensive log cabin in New England on the island. The Folwell family owned the island until it was acquired by the town of Islesboro in lieu of taxes. The town then sold it to the State of Maine for $1.00 in 1958, with the condition that it be used for recreational purposes. On June 30, 1967, Warren Island was officially dedicated as a State Park. Governor Kenneth Curtis and 40 state and local officials participated in the ceremony, which took place at around 4 p.m. Despite the threat of rain, everyone enjoyed a dinner of lobster, clams, pie, and coffee after the ceremony. From 1968 to 1983, Mr. Malcolm Graf served as the first Park Manager before being lost at sea. Known as "Mac," he established a tradition of thoughtful management, prioritizing the safe enjoyment of all visitors and campers on the island. Mac diligently upheld State Park rules while recognizing human fallibility. The current management aims to continue in the tradition established by him. Serenity perfectly describes this park covered in spruce trees, hidden away in Penobscot Bay. Visitors must use their own boats to access the island, as there is no public ferry service.

Campers can choose from 12 campsites or three Adirondack shelters for their accommodations. There is no landline phone on the island. However, cellphone service is generally reliable. The hiking trail, spanning 1.5 miles, covers the entire 70-acre island adorned with spruce trees, providing scenic views of Penobscot Bay and the nearby Camden Hills. Warren Island is a haven for birdwatchers, offering sightings of various bird species that are not easily spotted on the mainland. In recent years, multiple pairs of ospreys have made the island their seasonal home, constructing their nests high up in the trees. While it's delightful to observe these birds from a distance, it's important to respect their territorial rights, especially when they have young chicks in the nest. Great Horned Owls, though rarely seen, can often be heard with their eerie calls during the night. The park is home to a diverse range of bird species including blue herons, seagulls, ducks, loons, cormorants, sandpipers, woodpeckers, and many more. During your hike through this picturesque State Park, you may come across remnants of several houses from the past. On the southern end of the island, there is a beach where the water, though cold, is exceptionally clear. The park is open from 9:00 a.m. until sunset every day between Memorial Day and September 15. A fee is required for entry, and only cash or check payments are accepted. Credit cards are not accepted. Due to an increase in the number of vehicles seeking to use the parking lot at the Lincolnville Ferry Terminal, only ferry customers will be allowed to purchase parking passes. Previously granted waivers will no longer be issued. Park staff encourages park visitors and campers to take the ferry, find alternative parking in Lincolnville or launch their boats in Belfast. Visitors can access the island through the pier located on the eastern shore. A limited number of courtesy moorings are available for larger boats on a first-come, first-served basis. Park staff are not authorized to transport visitors unless in case of an emergency. Upon arrival, visitors should register at the open-air Visitors Information Center near the pier. Campers can use courtesy carts to transport their gear to the campsites. Please note that some campsites are reservable through the State Park Reservation System at www.campwithme.com and may be marked as already claimed for the night. Camping is only allowed on designated and marked campsites provided by the park. Caution should be exercised when handling fire. Fires are permitted only in designated fire pits and grills provided by the park, and no special permits are required. Visitors may collect firewood on the island but should refrain from disturbing live vegetation. As there are no public services on the island, visitors are responsible for carrying out all their generated trash during their visit. This includes organic and non-burnable trash from camping. Drinking water is available at the pier and in the middle of the island. Visitors are urged to protect the water supply by bathing and washing dishes away from these water sources. Warren Island is regularly patrolled by park rangers during the operating season from Memorial Day to September 15. However, there may be times when staff is unavailable to provide assistance. Visitors are encouraged to familiarize themselves with emergency procedures posted at the Visitors Information Center. Please be aware that Warren Island does not have standard utilities such as telephone service or electricity. In case of emergency, if you are unable to reach Warren Island staff at (207) 446-7090, you can contact rangers at Camden Hills State Park at 207-236-3109 to relay emergency messages for island campers.

NOTES:

PASSPORT STAMPS

WOLFE'S NECK WOODS STATE PARK

COUNTY: CUMBERLAND	ESTABLISHED: 1972	AREA (AC/HA): 245 / 99
DATE VISITED:	LODGING:	WHO I WENT WITH:
WEATHER: ☀☐ ☁☐ ☷☐ ❄☐ ☔☐ ☁☐		SPRING ☐ SUMMER ☐ FALL ☐ WINTER ☐
FEE(S):	RATING: ☆ ☆ ☆ ☆ ☆	WILL I RETURN? YES / NO

Established in 1972, Wolfe's Neck Woods State Park owes its existence to the generous donation of over 200 acres of diverse ecosystems by Mr. and Mrs. Lawrence M. C. Smith from Freeport. The donated land encompasses a range of natural habitats, including majestic climax white pine and hemlock forests, a salt marsh estuary, and the rugged coastlines of Casco Bay and the Harraseeket River. Situated on a wooded peninsula, known as the "neck," between the Harraseeket River and Casco Bay, the park derives its name from Henry and Rachel Woolfe, the first European settlers who made this area their permanent home in 1733. They, along with their descendants, cleared much of the peninsula to make way for farming, but over time, nature reclaimed this land, transforming it back into a thriving forest. Today, as a state park, this 245-acre expanse welcomes approximately 70,000 visitors annually, providing them with an opportunity to immerse themselves in the great outdoors and gain a deeper understanding of the natural world, fulfilling the aspirations of Mr. and Mrs. Smith. The park boasts five miles of walking trails, including a path that is accessible for wheelchairs and strollers, allowing people of all ages and abilities to explore the outdoors. There are plenty of quiet areas where you can rest, read a book, or enjoy a picnic by the shore, in the mowed field, or at a designated picnic site. The park provides amenities such as charcoal grills, restrooms, a drinking fountain, and a picnic shelter that can accommodate up to 60 people and can be reserved for a fee. The park is open throughout the year, from 9:00 a.m. until sunset, unless there are specific signs indicating otherwise at the entrance gate. Each season at Wolfe's Neck Woods State Park brings its own unique pleasures. During the spring season, the park hosts an annual birdwatching festival called "Spring Feathers over Freeport." Bird enthusiasts can enjoy observing ospreys as they arrive and begin nesting. The woods come alive with the emergence of wildflowers, including mayflowers and lady slippers. Nature programs are available on weekends at 2:00 p.m., weather permitting. In the summer, daily nature programs take place at 2:00 p.m. from mid-June through Labor Day, as long as the weather allows. Visitors can relish in the refreshing sea breezes, take leisurely walks in the shade, or have a delightful family picnic. As autumn arrives, the park displays a vibrant array of fall colors, although the intensity and timing of the foliage may vary from year to year. Similar to spring, nature programs are offered on weekends at 2:00 p.m., weather permitting. During winter, the park's gentle trails become perfect for snowshoers to explore. Nature programs continue on Sundays at 2:00 p.m., as long as the weather permits. The park offers several walks. Starting from the first parking lot: Fastest Route to the Water - Covering a distance of 0.1 mile, follow the path indicated by the sign "To Shore &

Casco Bay." Within 5 minutes, you will be able to appreciate the scenic beauty of the bay. Harraseeket Hike - This is a 1.8-mile loop trail with sections of steep and uneven terrain. Begin by entering the woods through the trail on the right side of the information kiosk located at the end of the first parking lot. Take the first right onto the Harraseeket Trail and continue along it as it traverses the woods, crossing the Old Woods Road Trail, Power Line Trail, and Wolf Neck Road (unpaved). After a gradual descent, the trail follows the cliffs overlooking the Harraseeket River, offering views of South Freeport. The trail then ascends, crosses Wolf Neck Road (paved), and passes the southern ends of the Hemlock Ridge, Old Woods Road, and Ledge Trails. It goes over two small hills before reaching the shoreline. From there, you can take the Casco Bay Trail to the left, which will lead you back to the parking lot. Woods and Water, Your Way - This is a 1.0 to 1.5-mile loop with some uneven terrain. Begin by entering the woods through the trail of your choice: Ledge Trail (shortest loop), Old Woods Road Trail (most level), or Hemlock Ridge Trail (longest loop). Once your chosen trail comes to an end, turn left and follow the Harraseeket Trail to reach the rocky shoreline and tidal beach along Casco Bay. Then, return via the Casco Bay Trail. From the second parking lot: Osprey Tour - This is a one-way route covering 0.2 mile. Start by passing the accessible bathrooms, fountain, and picnic sites. Follow the path as it curves through the field until you reach the White Pines Trail along the shore. Turn right and keep an eye out for birds in the woods and on the bay. Continue along the shore until you reach panel #4, which provides information about the estuary that supports the ospreys. Follow the trail further to reach the sign and benches across from Googins Island, where you have a good chance of observing osprey activity from April to August. (Walkers can access the rocky shore below via stone steps.) Forest and Shore Tour - This is a 0.75-mile loop trail with benches along the way for resting and enjoying the forest and shoreline. From the second parking lot, take the White Pines Trail into the shaded woods, where you'll encounter wildflowers and the songs of birds in season. At the 4-way junction with the North Loop Trail, turn right to stay on the accessible path that leads toward the bay. Keep an eye out for woodpecker holes in the trees and chipmunk holes near the trail. Along the bay, watch for ducks, gulls, and wading birds. At panel #5, observe ospreys from April to August. (Steps are available for walkers to access the rocky shore and Casco Bay Trail.) To return to the parking lot, retrace your steps and take the path across the field. Casco Bay Walk - This is a round trip of 1.25 miles. Starting from the second parking lot, take the White Pines Trail until you reach the 4-way junction with the North Loop Trail. Turn right and continue on the accessible path toward the bay. Follow the trail to panel #3 and descend the stairs to explore the salt marsh and mud flat. Proceed along the White Pines Trail to reach panel #4 and then panel #5, where you can observe ospreys. During low tide, you can walk down the stone steps to observe the tide pools. Walk along the rocks to the right and at the rocky shore panel (#6), take the rocky steps up to the junction with the Casco Bay Trail. Turn left and follow the Casco Bay Trail for approximately 0.25 mile to reach panel #7. Continue another 0.25 mile to panel #8, where you can enjoy views of the islands and access the rocky shore and tidal beach during low tide. Return using the same trail or by taking a forest trail. Handicap Accessible Trail: White Pines Trail - This trail is accessible and suitable for visitors in wheelchairs, with strollers, or those seeking level footing. It provides access to the osprey overlook and interpretive panels #1 and 3-5. To create a loop hike, start from the end of the second parking lot and follow the trail in a northward direction before looping eastward toward the shoreline. Wolfe's Neck Woods State Park is experiencing ecological changes due to the impact of the Hemlock woolly adelgid on Maine's forests. The Hemlock woolly adelgid is an invasive insect species that feeds on Eastern hemlock trees and typically causes their death within a decade. After years of feeding on hemlock trees in the park, often unnoticed, many trees are now severely weakened and dying. Although the Maine Forest Service has released predatory beetles to control the woolly adelgid, it is expected that most of the hemlock trees in Wolfe's Neck State Park will be killed within the next ten years. The loss of hemlock trees will have long-term consequences for the forest's ecology. Wolfe's Neck Woods State Park is situated in the Greater Portland & Casco Bay Region, offering a variety of attractions in the surrounding areas. Here are some other destinations worth exploring: Bradbury Mountain State Park: Located on Route 9 just north of the intersection with Elmwood Rd, this park spans 800 acres of forested land. It provides opportunities for camping, hiking, biking, and picnicking. For more information, visit www.maine.gov/bradburymountain. Eagle Island State Historic Site: Recognized as a National Historic Landmark, this site was once the summer residence of Adm. Robert E. Peary, an explorer of the North Pole. Situated about 3 miles off the coast of Harpswell, the island is accessible only by boat. For details, visit www.maine.gov/eagleisland. Crescent Beach State Park: Offering a pristine beach experience, this park is known for bathing in the surf or soaking up the sun on one of Maine's finest beaches. It is located approximately 8 miles south of Portland on Route 77 in Cape Elizabeth. Adjacent to Crescent Beach is Two Lights State Park. For more information, visit www.maine.gov/crescentbeach or www.maine.gov/twolights. Sebago Lake State Park: Nestled in Maine's Lakes & Mountains Region, this park features hiking trails, sandy beaches, picnic areas, a boat ramp, and a campground. It can be found off Route 302 in Casco & Naples. To learn more, visit www.maine.gov/sebagolake.

NOTES:

PASSPORT STAMPS

BIBLE POINT STATE HISTORIC SITE

COUNTY: PENOBSCOT   ESTABLISHED: 1971   AREA (AC/HA): 27 / 11

DATE VISITED: LODGING: WHO I WENT WITH:

WEATHER: ☀☐ ☁☐ ☔☐ ❄☐ ☁☐ ☁☐   SPRING ☐ SUMMER ☐ FALL ☐ WINTER ☐

FEE(S):   RATING: ☆ ☆ ☆ ☆ ☆   WILL I RETURN? YES / NO

A 27-acre property located near the southern end of Mattawamkeag Lake gained fame through its association with Teddy Roosevelt, who first visited the area in 1878. As a young man, guided by his lifelong friend and guide Bill Sewall, Roosevelt would camp at the southern end of Mattawamkeag Lake and engage in hunting and fishing activities throughout the region. It is said that each day, Roosevelt would take his bible and hike to a picturesque point of land where the West Branch of the Mattawamkeag River and First Brook meet. There, he would spend time reading the bible. A plaque, erected in 1921 by Roosevelt's biographer Hermann Hagedorn, now stands at the site to commemorate Roosevelt's deep affection for the area. The inscription on the plaque reads: "This place, to which a great man in his youth liked to come to commune with God and with the wonder and beauty of the visible world, is dedicated to the happy memory of THEODORE ROOSEVELT. Stranger, rest here and consider what one man, having faith in the right and love for his fellow man was able to do for his country." In 1970, Bible Point was designated as a historic place on the State Register. In December 1971, this site was donated to the State of Maine for preservation as a natural area.

NOTES:

PASSPORT STAMPS

COLBURN HOUSE STATE HISTORIC SITE

COUNTY: KENNEBEC	ESTABLISHED: 1971	AREA (AC/HA): 6 / 2.4
DATE VISITED:	LODGING:	WHO I WENT WITH:
WEATHER: ☼☐ ☁☐ ☷☐ ❄☐ ☔☐ ☁☐		SPRING ☐ SUMMER ☐ FALL ☐ WINTER ☐
FEE(S):	RATING: ☆ ☆ ☆ ☆ ☆	WILL I RETURN? YES / NO

The grounds of the property are open from 9:00 a.m. until sunset every day. However, access to the Colburn House, carriage house, and barn is limited to special events. While it is true that George Washington never stayed at this house, he was acquainted with its owner. However, two other notable figures from the American Revolution did spend nights here—Benedict Arnold and Aaron Burr. Constructed in 1765, this colonial Federal-style house served as the residence for multiple generations of the influential Colburn family. In September 1775, Colonel Benedict Arnold led a military expedition consisting of over 1,000 colonial soldiers up the Kennebec River with the objective of attacking the British stronghold of Quebec City. These men, who had traveled from Massachusetts on eleven ships, disembarked at the home of Reuben Colburn, a member of the Maine Committee of Safety. Colburn had played a crucial role in conceptualizing the idea of launching an attack on British-held Quebec through the Maine wilderness. He had also provided vital information to General Washington. Upon Arnold's arrival, Colburn had already prepared 200 wooden boats called bateaux, which were used to transport provisions and military supplies upstream towards Canada. The Colburn House served as Arnold's headquarters and the starting point for his famous expedition against Quebec. In addition to his contributions, Colburn had gathered a skilled crew and managed to construct the boats within a mere two weeks of General Washington's request. However, due to a shortage of seasoned lumber, the builders had to resort to using green wood, which was more susceptible to water damage. Twenty of these craftsmen, including Colburn himself, accompanied the expedition to Canada, carrying supplies and conducting repairs on the boats throughout the journey.

NOTES:

PASSPORT STAMPS

COLONIAL PEMAQUID STATE HISTORIC SITE (FT. WILLIAM HENRY)

COUNTY: LINCOLN	ESTABLISHED: 1969	AREA (AC/HA): 24 / 9

DATE VISITED:	LODGING:	WHO I WENT WITH:

WEATHER: ☼☐ ☁☐ ☁☐ ❄☐ ☂☐ ☁☐	SPRING ☐ SUMMER ☐ FALL ☐ WINTER ☐

FEE(S):	RATING: ☆ ☆ ☆ ☆ ☆	WILL I RETURN? YES / NO

The land of Pemaquid was inhabited by Native Americans long before Europeans arrived. The Native tribes in this region, namely the Wabanaki and Etchemen, were already living here when English fishermen began establishing their fishing stations in the early 1610s. The interactions and relationships between the Native Americans and Europeans played a significant role in the region's development and politics during the 17th and 18th centuries. These interactions continue to have an impact even today. Pemaquid, founded between 1625 and 1628, stands as one of the earliest and historically important English settlements in the country. Located next to a small harbor, it served as England's farthest outpost in the northeastern region. Being the closest settlement to the French in Acadia, several forts were constructed here to safeguard the settlers from French attacks and to establish a strong presence for the protection of southern New England. Pemaquid experienced early success and rapid growth. Its economy relied on fishing, fur trade with Native Americans, timber, and agriculture. However, the English government failed to provide effective defenses for Pemaquid, leading to its abandonment twice during a series of prolonged Colonial wars that erupted along the Maine coast from 1676 onwards. Despite the challenges faced by the settlers, they left behind significant evidence of their lives on the frontier during the 1600s and 1700s. This evidence has been unearthed through a series of archaeological investigations that commenced in 1965. The findings from this research, displayed in the museum and on the grounds of Colonial Pemaquid, offer a valuable glimpse into New England frontier life 375 years ago. In 1677, Fort Charles was constructed in this area to safeguard an English settlement that had already suffered destruction once during the initial French and Indian Wars. The fort, featuring seven cannons and walls made of wooden pickets, seemed to be a formidable defensive structure in this rugged and volatile frontier, which was claimed by both England and France. However, despite its outward strength, Fort Charles was captured in 1689 during an attack by Native Americans, who were encouraged by their French allies. The fort's garrison, plagued by desertions and consisting of as few as 16 men, was insufficient in size. Furthermore, enemy fire from a nearby rock outcrop posed a particularly lethal and challenging threat to counter. The devastation and desertion of Fort Charles and the Pemaquid settlement marked a significant triumph for the Native Americans and their French allies. Consequently, England relinquished control over mid-coast Maine for the following three years. Constructed in 1692, Fort William Henry was an exceptional feat of engineering for its time. Governor Sir William Phips of Massachusetts allocated a significant portion of the colony's funds to build this fortification. The construction involved the use of 2,000 cartloads of stone to erect walls ranging from

10 to 22 feet in height, as well as a towering stone bastion standing at 29 feet. The fort was equipped with nearly 20 cannons and housed a garrison of 60 soldiers. However, despite its impressive appearance, the fort's durability was short-lived. In 1696, Native tribes, who were aggrieved by their mistreatment at the hands of the English, joined forces once again with the French to launch an attack on Fort William Henry. Despite its initial appearance of strength, the fort proved to be vulnerable. The mortar used in constructing the stone walls was of subpar quality and proved incapable of withstanding the assault. Consequently, Fort William Henry succumbed to the attack, and the English were forced to abandon Pemaquid once more. Fort Frederick was constructed in 1729, a significant 33 years after the downfall of Fort William Henry. Colonel David Dunbar, who held the position of Surveyor of His Majesty's Woods in America, spearheaded the re-establishment of a settlement in this area. Dunbar brought in recent immigrants from Boston, primarily Scots-Irish, to populate the settlement and oversee the reconstruction of the fort. However, Dunbar faced opposition from the Massachusetts government, which disputed his authority to grant land titles to the new settlers. Following a legal battle with Massachusetts, Dunbar and the settlers ultimately abandoned Pemaquid. Massachusetts then dispatched a garrison to Fort Frederick and maintained control over the fort until 1759 when it was decommissioned. Over time, Fort Frederick fell into disrepair. In 1775, local residents made the decision to demolish it to prevent its occupation by British troops during the American Revolution. The construction of the Fort House took place in the final quarter of the 18th century. Its name derives from its close proximity to the remains of Fort Frederick. The only notable connection it had with the forts was that its earliest recorded owner, Alexander Nickels Jr., was the son of one of Fort Frederick's final commanders. This house served as the farmhouse for a 300-acre farm that encompassed the "village" area of Colonial Pemaquid, featuring pastures for livestock and fields for crops. It was not until the 1960s, when archaeological investigations were carried out on Colonial Pemaquid, that we began to gain insights into the possible lifestyles of the European settlers and Native Americans who resided here during the 17th and 18th centuries. The museum, a replica of a 17th-century fisherman's dwelling, the Fort House, and the forts are accessible to visitors from 9:00 a.m. to 5:00 p.m. daily during the period from Memorial Day to Labor Day. There is an admission fee for entry. However, even during the off-season, visitors are welcome to enjoy the park grounds from 9:00 a.m. until sunset. It's important to note that the buildings and facilities are closed during the off-season. The Museum/Visitor Center provides informative displays about the history of Pemaquid, covering a range of topics from the early Native American presence to the Colonial era. It showcases a curated collection of artifacts, carefully selected from over 100,000 items excavated at this site. Additionally, visitors can explore a detailed diorama of the Pemaquid Village, offering a visual representation of the settlement. To engage children and enhance their museum experience, there are museum searches available, designed as a scavenger hunt-style activity. Restrooms are conveniently located within the Museum for visitors' convenience. Located just down the hill from Fort William Henry, on the waterfront dock, is the

Contented Sole restaurant. This local favorite not only offers delicious food but also serves as a gathering place for many of the programs organized by the Friends of Colonial Pemaquid. As one of northern New England's earliest communities with a rich archaeological history, Colonial Pemaquid State Historic Site is a must-visit destination when exploring Midcoast Maine. The knowledgeable staff from the Bureau of Parks and Lands conduct interpretive tours, providing insights into the native people who once camped on this secluded peninsula that eventually transformed into a rugged frontier settlement dating back to the mid-1620s. The museum showcases unearthed artifacts, including exquisite china patterns, a 400-year-old trunk, a rare German Bellarmine jug, and various tools from that era, offering a glimpse into village life. After exploring the grounds, make sure to visit Fort William Henry and take in the panoramic view from its roof. Through the telescope, imagine what it was like in the 17th century, guarding the waters of the Pemaquid River and beyond. The Fort House, constructed in the late 18th century by Alexander Nickels Jr., the son of the last commander of Fort Frederick, is another notable site. Today, the first floor of the Fort House is open to the public, featuring a period room or parlor decorated in a style reminiscent of the early 1800s, a library, an exhibit room, and an archaeological laboratory. The Village comprises a collection of 14 stone cellar holes that provide insight into the location and purpose of several structures from different periods in the village's history. Many of these cellar holes feature interpretive panels describing the likely function of the building and showcasing artifacts discovered during archaeological excavations. The Cemetery houses gravestones that date back as early as the 1700s. While privately owned, the Maine Bureau of Parks and Lands assists in its preservation. As many of the gravestones are fragile, visitors are kindly requested not to make rubbings from them. For additional information about specific gravestones, inventory sheets can be obtained at the Fort House. Visitors have access to the Pier and Boat Ramp, allowing them to launch their boats into Pemaquid Harbor for coastal tours of Pemaquid, South Bristol, Boothbay, New Harbor, and Chamberlain. Alternatively, fishing for mackerel off the pier is also an option for a day's activity. Picnic areas are conveniently located throughout various sections of the park, providing pleasant spots for outdoor meals.

NOTES:

PASSPORT STAMPS

EAGLE ISLAND STATE HISTORIC SITE

COUNTY: CUMBERLAND   ESTABLISHED: 1967   AREA (AC/HA): 17 / 6

DATE VISITED: LODGING: WHO I WENT WITH:

WEATHER: ☀☐ ☁☐ 🌫☐ ❄☐ 🌦☐ 🌫☐   SPRING ☐ SUMMER ☐ FALL ☐ WINTER ☐

FEE(S):   RATING: ☆ ☆ ☆ ☆ ☆   WILL I RETURN? YES / NO

Eagle Island is situated within the town of Harpswell, located in Cumberland County, approximately 12 miles northeast of Portland. It is a 17-acre island positioned in the outermost region of the Casco Bay island chain. As part of Harpswell administratively, it is situated 12 miles northeast of Portland and 15 miles south of Brunswick. The island reaches a maximum elevation of 40 feet above sea level and is characterized by rocky terrain with a thin layer of topsoil. The majority of the island is covered in coniferous trees and brush, with trails providing access to most areas. Historic Landmark attract approximately 6,000 visitors each season. It serves as the summer residence of Admiral Robert Peary, renowned for his exploration of the North Pole. At the northern end of the island, there is a Y-shaped clearing where the main structures are situated, including the Peary house, a cabin for the caretaker, and a visitors center. Adjacent to this area, there is a small beach with a long wooden pier. The pier was constructed in 1969, while the visitors center was added in 2012. The island was acquired in 1881 for a mere $200 and offers a picturesque location for Peary's summer home, commanding views of Casco Bay and the surrounding islands. Recognizing its national significance in American history, Eagle Island received National Historic Landmark designation on August 25, 2014, conferred by the Secretary of the Interior. The Peary House is a wooden-framed residence that was constructed in multiple stages. The original section of the house was built in 1904 and consisted of a rectangular structure with a spacious living room on the first floor and three bedrooms on the second floor. Meals were prepared in a separate caretaker's house, which proved to be insufficient, leading to the addition of a small kitchen and dining wing in 1906. To enhance the foundation, a new fieldstone foundation with concrete piers was installed, raising the structure to include a full-height basement. Shed-roof dormers were also added to both sides of the gabled roof. Following his retirement, Admiral Peary further expanded the building in 1912-1913. The 1906 kitchen wing was detached, and an expanded wing with a porch on three sides was constructed. Additionally, Admiral Peary built two circular stone bastions, which served the dual purpose of retaining walls to protect the house from stormy weather and housing his collection of artifacts from his numerous expeditions. After Admiral Peary's passing in 1920, his family made only minor modifications to the house before eventually donating the property to the state in 1967. The state took on the responsibility of building the pier and restoring the property, which had suffered from weather-related deterioration. In 1990, a section of the roof of the Peary House collapsed, resulting in water damage to Peary's study and necessitating its reconstruction. Guests visiting Eagle Island are treated to panoramic vistas of the ocean, the cries of seagulls, and the scents of blooming flowers, providing a unique opportunity to experience a day in the life of the celebrated explorer from the early 1900s. The island remains untouched by modern mechanical devices, creating an atmosphere where one can imagine Admiral Peary and his wife, Josephine, sitting atop the library's roof, observing visitors as they explore different corners of their island retreat. Josephine, known for her gardening prowess, cultivated exquisite flower beds that featured vibrant foxgloves and other colorful blooms. Today, the gardens are meticulously maintained by the staff of the Bureau of Parks and Lands. The site provides a variety of activities for visitors to enjoy, including boating (motorized), fishing, hiking, and sea kayaking. While in the vicinity, it is highly recommended to also visit the Peary-McMillan Arctic Museum at Bowdoin College in Brunswick. Admiral Peary himself was an alumnus of Bowdoin College, making the museum an excellent complement to the exploration of Eagle Island. Those arriving at Eagle Island by their own watercraft are asked to contact Eagle Island staff for mooring and anchoring instructions. You can contact them via VHF-FM channel 9. Alternatively, you can proceed directly to the float located at the end of the pier.

NOTES:

PASSPORT STAMPS

FORT BALDWIN STATE HISTORIC SITE

COUNTY: SAGADAHOC	ESTABLISHED: 1979	AREA (AC/HA): 6 / 2.4

DATE VISITED:	LODGING:	WHO I WENT WITH:

WEATHER: ☀☐ ⛅☐ ☔☐ ❄☐ ⛈☐ 🌫☐   SPRING ☐ SUMMER ☐ FALL ☐ WINTER ☐

FEE(S):   RATING: ☆ ☆ ☆ ☆ ☆   WILL I RETURN? YES / NO

The operating hours of Fort Baldwin are from May 1 to September 30, starting at 9:00 a.m. and ending at sunset, unless there are any specific notices posted at the entrance indicating otherwise. Please note that there are no facilities available at the site. Visitors are welcome to explore the grounds during the off-season, but it's important to be aware that the trail to the Fort is not cleared of snow. Fort Baldwin, named after Jeduthan Baldwin, who served as an engineer for the Colonial army during the Revolutionary War, was constructed between 1905 and 1912. Battery Cogan was equipped with two 3-inch M1903 guns mounted on pedestals. It was named after a lieutenant who served in the 5th Continental Regiment during the American Revolution. Lieutenant Cogan, who also held the position of quartermaster in the 1st New Hampshire Regiment, passed away on August 21, 1778. Battery Joseph Roswell Hawley housed two 6-inch M1900 guns on pedestal mounts. This battery also served as the fort's original observation station and contained electric equipment. It was named in honor of Brigadier General Joseph R. Hawley, who achieved great distinction during the American Civil War. Battery Hardman featured one 6-inch gun M1905 on a disappearing carriage. It was named after Captain Hardman, who served in the 2nd Maryland Regiment of the Continental Army during the American Revolution. Captain Hardman was taken as a prisoner at Camden, South Carolina, and sadly lost his life while in captivity on September 1, 1780. Furthermore, Fort Popham, located nearby, had facilities for a controlled minefield in the river. Prior to the United States' entry into World War I, Fort Baldwin was in a caretaker status and likely fell under the command of the Coast Defenses of the Kennebec. During World War I, both Fort Baldwin and Fort Popham were manned by a garrison of 200 soldiers from the 13th and 29th Coast Artillery companies, which were part of the Coast Defenses of Portland. In 1917, all three 6-inch guns at Fort Baldwin were removed as part of a program to mount these weapons on field carriages for use on the Western Front. The guns from Battery Hawley were not deployed overseas and were reinstalled in 1919. The gun from Battery Hardman was sent to France, and although it eventually returned to the United States, it was not returned to Fort Baldwin. According to a history of the Coast Artillery in World War I, none of the regiments in France equipped with 6-inch guns completed their training in time to participate in combat before the Armistice. In 1924, Fort Baldwin was disarmed as part of a larger reduction in coastal defense systems and was subsequently sold to the State of Maine. At the beginning of World War II, four circular concrete "Panama mounts" were constructed at Fort Baldwin, with two of them placed on Battery Hawley's former 6-inch gun positions. These mounts were intended to provide improved firing platforms for towed 155 mm

M1918 guns, which were adopted by the Coast Artillery after World War I. From 1941 to 1943, Battery D of the 8th Coast Artillery manned Fort Baldwin and protected its Fire Control Tower, which could transmit the precise location of enemy vessels to batteries in Casco Bay, notably Battery Steele with its 16-inch guns. A battery consisting of four 155 mm guns, likely from Fort Williams, was deployed to Fort Baldwin from early 1942 until January 17, 1944. After the war, the Army returned the property to the State of Maine in 1949.

NOTES:

PASSPORT STAMPS

FORT EDGECOMB STATE HISTORIC SITE

COUNTY: LINCOLN   **ESTABLISHED:** 1969   **AREA (AC/HA):** 3 / 1.2

DATE VISITED:	**LODGING:**	**WHO I WENT WITH:**

WEATHER: ☀☐ ☁☐ ☔☐ ❄☐ ⛈☐ 🌫☐   SPRING ☐ SUMMER ☐ FALL ☐ WINTER ☐

FEE(S):   **RATING:** ☆ ☆ ☆ ☆ ☆   **WILL I RETURN?** YES / NO

Fort Edgecomb State Historic Site in Edgecomb, Maine holds a special place in the local community's history and pride. While it never faced any significant battles, it has become a cherished gathering spot for entertainment, family, and community events. Although it may not be renowned for its military achievements, it remains a beloved destination for the locals. Constructed in 1808, Fort Edgecomb is a two-story octagonal wooden blockhouse situated on David Island, within the town of Edgecomb. Recognized as a historic site, it was added to the National Register of Historic Places in 1969. In 1991, its boundaries were expanded to establish a larger "historic district." Originally built to protect Wiscasset, a vital shipping center north of Boston, Fort Edgecomb was designed with eight sides to provide a panoramic view of the surrounding area and defend against both water and land attacks. While it played a role in the War of 1812, it never saw any actual combat until 1814, when British forces turned their attention toward America after Napoleon's power was diminished. However, the cannons at Fort Edgecomb were only fired on one occasion—to celebrate James Madison's inauguration as President of the United States. Despite lacking a significant military history, local residents have passionately worked to preserve the blockhouse and its surroundings for centuries. In 1875, they organized their first fundraiser to prevent the fort's destruction. Eventually, Governor Percival Baxter purchased the fort and adjacent land from the Federal Government in 1923 for a mere $501. Today, the fort continues to serve as a park that hosts various events, including theater performances and musicals. It is frequently rented for weddings and family reunions, thanks to its stunning views. Visitors can spend time enjoying the waterfront, where they can observe playful harbor seals, witness lobster boats passing by, and catch glimpses of nesting osprey. With its picturesque scenery, it's no surprise that the fort is a popular location for picnics and leisurely days in the sun. The meticulous preservation of the fort adds to its allure, making it a truly remarkable destination.

NOTES:

PASSPORT STAMPS

FORT HALIFAX STATE HISTORIC SITE

COUNTY: KENNEBEC	ESTABLISHED: 1968	AREA (AC/HA): - / -

DATE VISITED: **LODGING:**   **WHO I WENT WITH:**

WEATHER: ☀☐ ☁☐ ☷☐ ❄☐ ☔☐ ☁☐   SPRING ☐ SUMMER ☐ FALL ☐ WINTER ☐

FEE(S):   **RATING:** ☆ ☆ ☆ ☆ ☆   **WILL I RETURN?** YES / NO

Fort Halifax is a historic British colonial outpost situated on the banks of the Sebasticook River near its confluence with the Kennebec River. Initially constructed as a wooden palisaded fort in 1754 during the French and Indian War, only one blockhouse remains today. This blockhouse holds the distinction of being the oldest blockhouse in the United States. It has been preserved as the Fort Halifax State Historic Site and is open to the public during the warmer months. The primary purpose of the fort was to protect the Wabanaki canoe routes that connected the St. Lawrence and Penobscot Valleys, utilizing the Chaudière-Kennebec and Sebasticook-Souadabscook rivers. These waterways were vital for transportation and trade. The surviving blockhouse serves as a testament to the fort's historical significance. Recognizing its historical and cultural importance, the blockhouse was designated as a National Historic Landmark and added to the National Register of Historic Places in 1968. Visitors have the opportunity to explore the site and learn about its rich history. Unfortunately, on April 1, 1987, the fort fell victim to severe flooding, as the waters rose to a height of eight feet, completely demolishing the structure. The scattered log timbers were eventually recovered by crews in boats, even finding pieces miles downriver. The following year, the blockhouse was meticulously reconstructed. Today, the fort proudly holds the distinction of being recognized as a National Historic Landmark.

NOTES:

PASSPORT STAMPS

FORT KENT STATE HISTORIC SITE

COUNTY: AROOSTOOK	ESTABLISHED: 1969	AREA (AC/HA): - / -

DATE VISITED: **LODGING:**   **WHO I WENT WITH:**

WEATHER: ☀☐ ☁☐ ☷☐ ❄☐ ☔☐ ☲☐   SPRING ☐ SUMMER ☐ FALL ☐ WINTER ☐

FEE(S):   **RATING:** ☆ ☆ ☆ ☆ ☆   **WILL I RETURN?** YES / NO

Fort Kent, situated in the town of Fort Kent, Maine, where the Fish and Saint John rivers meet, stands as the sole remaining American fortification constructed during the Aroostook War, a period of border tensions with neighboring New Brunswick. Today, it is preserved as the Fort Kent State Historic Site, showcasing an authentic log blockhouse that is accessible for tours during the summer months. Recognizing its historical significance, the fort was listed on the National Register of Historic Places in 1969 and designated as a National Historic Landmark in 1973. Fort Kent is situated on a small elevation, providing a vantage point overlooking the Saint John River. It is located just west of the mouth of the Fish River. In this area, the Saint John River serves as part of the border between Canada and the United States. Prior to the 1842 Webster-Ashburton Treaty, the territory on both sides of the river was subject to dispute between the United States and the United Kingdom, with New Brunswick being a colonial province of the UK at the time. The remaining structure of Fort Kent is a two-story blockhouse, measuring approximately 23 feet 5 inches (7.14 m) on each side. It is constructed using hand-hewn cedar timbers and features an overhanging second story with a pyramidal roof. Each side of the roof has a gabled dormer. The main entrance faces west and is accompanied by four rifle ports on the first floor. Additionally, there are twelve rifle ports on the first floor of the other three sides. The second floor, which extends 15 inches (0.38 m) beyond the first floor, has eleven rifle ports on the east and west sides, and fifteen on the north and south sides. On the first floor, there are two cannon ports on both the north and south sides. The interior of the blockhouse has undergone minor modifications to accommodate heating, plumbing, and museum displays. Following the Treaty of Paris in 1783, which recognized the United States, the boundary between Maine and New Brunswick became a recurring point of disagreement. While part of the eastern border was settled with the Jay Treaty of 1797, the upper Saint John River area remained a source of dispute. Both Maine and New Brunswick sought to develop the region to strengthen their claims, which led to escalating tensions from the 1820s onwards. Authorities from each government took action against settlers and agents of the other, further exacerbating the situation. As tensions reached their peak, the construction of Fort Kent commenced in 1838. The fort was named after Governor Edward Kent and was part of a series of forts built by the state along the southern banks of the Saint John River. It is the only fort that has survived (the blockhouse at Fort Fairfield is a reconstruction from the 20th century). In 1839, the arrest of a U.S. government agent in New Brunswick prompted Congress to authorize the deployment of 50,000 federal troops to northern Maine. During this time, the fort was expanded to include barracks, officers' quarters, and other buildings. General Winfield Scott was assigned to the area with the authority to negotiate a resolution. Scott, along with New Brunswick Lieutenant Governor John Harvey, who had a long-standing friendship, successfully managed to reduce tensions until the Webster-Ashburton Treaty was negotiated in 1842. United States troops remained stationed at the fort until 1845. After the crisis had passed, the fort was sold into private ownership. In 1891, the property was purchased by the state of Maine with the intention of establishing a park. However, substantive work on the site did not begin until 1959 when the historic site was officially established. The museum at the fort is now maintained by the Fort Kent Historical Society.

NOTES:

PASSPORT STAMPS

FORT KNOX STATE HISTORIC SITE

COUNTY: WALDO	ESTABLISHED: 1969	AREA (AC/HA): 125 / 50

DATE VISITED:	LODGING:	WHO I WENT WITH:

WEATHER: ☼□ ☁□ ☷□ ❄□ ☂□ ☕□	SPRING □ SUMMER □ FALL □ WINTER □

FEE(S):	RATING: ☆☆☆☆☆	WILL I RETURN? YES / NO

Fort Knox State Historic Site, is situated on the western side of the Penobscot River in Prospect. It is located approximately 5 miles (8.0 km) from the river's mouth. The fort was constructed between 1844 and 1869, and it holds the distinction of being the first fort in Maine to be built entirely of granite. Previous forts had utilized wood, earth, and stone in their construction. The fort was named after Major General Henry Knox, who served as the first U.S. Secretary of War and was a Commander of Artillery during the American Revolutionary War. Towards the end of his life, Knox resided not far from the fort in Thomaston. Fort Knox stands as an exceptionally well-preserved example of a granite coastal fortification from the mid-19th century. Its historical significance led to its inclusion on the National Register of Historic Places in 1969, and it was designated as a National Historic Landmark on December 30, 1970. In addition to its historical value, Fort Knox also serves as the entrance site for the observation tower of the Penobscot Narrows Bridge. This bridge, which opened to the public in 2007, provides visitors with breathtaking views of the surrounding area. The local collective memory of Maine's humiliation at the hands of the British during the American Revolution and the War of 1812 played a significant role in fostering anti-British sentiment in Eastern Maine. The Penobscot Expedition of 1779 was an attempt to expel the British from New Ireland (Maine), but it ended in a disastrous failure. The American forces lost 43 ships and suffered around 500 casualties, making it the most devastating naval defeat for the United States prior to the attack on Pearl Harbor during World War II. Then, in the autumn of 1814, during the War of 1812, a British naval fleet and soldiers sailed up the Penobscot River and defeated an outnumbered American force in the Battle of Hampden. Following their victory, the British troops looted both Hampden and Bangor. This defeat of the Americans further fueled the movement for Maine's statehood after the war, which was achieved in 1820 since Massachusetts had failed to adequately protect the region. The Aroostook War of 1838-1839 revived the anti-British sentiment and concerns about the vulnerability of the region to another attack similar to that of 1814. Additionally, the Penobscot Valley and Bangor were major sources of lumber for shipbuilding. As a response to these concerns, the Penobscot River was included in the Third System of coastal fortifications, leading to the construction of Fort Knox. This imposing granite fort, located at the mouth of the Penobscot River, was a significant investment and part of the efforts to safeguard the area. Construction of Fort Knox commenced in 1844 and continued until 1869 when all funding for masonry forts was withdrawn. During this period, the fort was mostly completed, except for the emplacements on the upper level known as the "roof" or barbette level. The funding from Congress was inconsistent, and as a result, the fort's design was never fully finished, despite a total expenditure of $1,000,000. The granite used for construction was quarried from Mount Waldo in Frankfort, located five miles (8 km) upriver. The overall design of the fort was overseen by Joseph G. Totten, a renowned engineer from the Army Corps of Engineers and a leading expert in fortification engineering at the time. Notable engineer officers who supervised the construction included Isaac Ingalls Stevens and Thomas L. Casey. In addition to the main fort, which housed 64 guns, Fort Knox featured two water batteries facing the river. Each battery was equipped with a shot furnace used to heat cannonballs to a temperature that would ignite wooden ships if the cannonball became lodged in the vessel. However, with the introduction of ironclad warships, these furnaces became obsolete. Fort Knox, despite its strategic location and military significance, never experienced any actual battles. However, it was manned during times of war. During the American Civil War, volunteers from Maine, who were primarily recruits undergoing training before being assigned to active duty, occupied the fort. Thomas Lincoln Casey, an engineer officer, supervised the ongoing work at the fort. He made adaptations to the batteries to accommodate the newly invented Rodman cannon and ensured the completion of the fort. In the subsequent conflict, the Spanish-American War, a regiment from Connecticut took charge of Fort Knox. A plaque at the fort commemorates the laying of a controlled minefield in the river during this war. Congress allocated $3,200 for this purpose shortly after the outbreak of the war, as mentioned on the plaque. Following the end of the war, the garrison at Fort Knox was reduced to a single individual known as the "Keeper of the Fort" or caretaker, holding the rank of ordnance sergeant. The primary responsibility of the keeper was to ensure the maintenance and upkeep of the fort. They reported to Fort Preble in South Portland. In 1900, a permanent structure called the "torpedo storehouse" was added to the fort. Originally used for storing naval mines, which were referred to as torpedoes at the time, this building now serves as the Visitor's Center. In 1923, the federal government declared Fort Knox as excess property and put its 125-acre grounds up for sale. The state of Maine purchased the fort for the sum of $2,121. Since 1943, it has been managed and maintained as a Maine state historic site. To transform the fort into a tourist destination, a work crew from the Ellsworth camp of the Civilian Conservation Corps (Co. 193) was deployed. They carried out various tasks, as reported in the November 1936 issue of Brann News, the camp newspaper. The accomplished work included creating a picnic area, reforesting the surrounding area, constructing roads, improving drainage within the fort, developing springs, building table and bench combinations, installing fireplaces, reconstructing the retaining wall along the river side of the fort, repairing masonry work, and making interior renovations to the fort. Fort Knox is renowned today as one of the best-preserved and most easily accessible forts in the United States. It offers extensive access to the public, allowing visitors to explore virtually all areas of the fort. The site houses various historical weapons from the period, including two 15-inch Rodman smoothbores located in the water batteries (one of which has been remounted), an 8-inch Rodman converted rifle near the parking lot, a 10-inch Rodman smoothbore within the fort, and several

24-pounder flank howitzers. There is a need for clarification regarding the exact number of flank howitzers. Some of these howitzers are mounted on original carriages, and the bronze plates on these carriages bear the inscription "Fort Monroe 1862." The remounted 15-inch Rodman guns are particularly rare, as they weigh a staggering 50,000 pounds. These guns were the largest weapons produced in significant quantities during the Civil War period.

NOTES:

PASSPORT STAMPS

FORT MCCLARY STATE HISTORIC SITE

COUNTY: YORK	ESTABLISHED: 1969		AREA (AC/HA): - / -
DATE VISITED:	LODGING:	WHO I WENT WITH:	
WEATHER: ☼☐ ☁☐ ☂☐ ❄☐ ☔☐ ☁☐		SPRING ☐ SUMMER ☐ FALL ☐ WINTER ☐	
FEE(S):	RATING: ☆☆☆☆☆	WILL I RETURN? YES / NO	

Fort McClary, situated at Kittery Point, Maine, was once a fortified defense system utilized by the United States military. Its strategic position along the southern coast, at the mouth of the Piscataqua River, served to safeguard the harbor of Portsmouth, New Hampshire, and the nearby Portsmouth Naval Shipyard in Kittery during the 19th century. Presently, the property, along with its remaining structures, is under the ownership and operation of the State of Maine as Fort McClary State Historic Site. Among the notable structures is a blockhouse dating back to 1844, offering a glimpse into the fort's historical significance. The origins of coastal defenses at the site of Fort McClary can be traced back to the late 17th century when William Pepperell, a prominent shipbuilder, acquired the property and constructed basic defensive structures in 1689. Prior to that, the village relied on Fort William and Mary in New Castle for protection. In 1715, the Province of Massachusetts Bay decided to establish a permanent breastwork armed with six cannons to defend the Piscataqua River, in preparation for the conflicts of Father Rale's War. Some sources suggest that the fortification aimed to safeguard Maine (then part of Massachusetts) from excessive taxes imposed by the governor of New Hampshire on citizens of neighboring colonies. Additionally, the fort was utilized to collect duties from Massachusetts residents for its own maintenance. In 1803, the fort, known as Fort William, was transferred to the United States government, although no surviving remnants of its features are known. During the American Revolution, the Pepperrells, who remained loyal to the British, had their property, including the fort, confiscated by local Patriot forces. In 1776, ammunition was provided for the fort's cannons, and the New Hampshire militia took control of the fort until 1779. Fort McClary was formally established in 1808 as a component of the second system of fortifications in the United States. It was named after Major Andrew McClary, a native of New Hampshire and an American officer who lost his life in the Battle of Bunker Hill in 1775. The fort comprised a semi-elliptical lower battery equipped with 9 or 10 guns and a shot furnace. Additionally, there was an upper battery located near the current blockhouse, but there is limited information available regarding its armament. Throughout the 19th century, Fort McClary remained in use, particularly during the War of 1812, although it did not witness any combat. During the 1840s, Fort McClary underwent further expansion, likely in response to tensions between the United States and Great Britain regarding the disputed border between Maine and New Brunswick. This period of expansion was influenced by the bloodless Aroostook War and the signing of the Webster-Ashburton Treaty in 1842. In 1844, the blockhouse was constructed near the former upper battery, marking the final blockhouse built at a fort in Maine and one of the last in coastal forts across the

United States. The fort played an active role during the American Civil War and underwent significant reconstruction under the third system of fortifications, which was never fully completed. At the onset of the war, the Maine Coast Guard and the Kittery Artillery company manned the fort, with the addition of the Maine State Guard in 1864. Notably, Vice President Hannibal Hamlin served as a private and a cook in the fort as part of the Maine State Guard. Despite its active use, Fort McClary saw minimal action during the Civil War. A major rebuilding and expansion initiative began in 1863, aiming to transform the fort into a large five-sided structure equipped with one or two tiers of cannons on all sides. However, only the seawalls on the two seaward fronts were completed, along with one of the landward cannon bastions featuring a granite magazine. To address the vulnerability of masonry forts to rifled cannons, which became evident during the war, funding for masonry fort projects was withdrawn in 1867. Consequently, Fort McClary had limited positions for cannons, and remnants of the fort's unfinished construction, including numerous granite blocks, can still be seen today. During the 1870s, the lower battery at Fort McClary underwent a rebuilding process that included the addition of three temporary gun positions for 10-inch Parrott rifles. However, funding for further improvements was once again halted, resulting in limited progress. In the 1890s, the fort stored nine 15-inch Rodman smoothbore guns and seven carriages, intended for mounting in the event of a war. Three of these Rodmans were mounted as an emergency measure during the Spanish-American War in 1898. However, the fort's significance diminished with the construction of Fort Foster in Kittery, Maine, and the establishment of new batteries at Fort Constitution as part of the Endicott Program by 1901. By the 1910s, most of Fort McClary had fallen into disrepair, leading to its official decommissioning in 1918. In 1924, the State of Maine acquired the majority of the fort's property from the federal government, subsequently managing it as a park. Over the following decades, several deteriorated structures were demolished. Parts of the fort were utilized by civilian defense forces during World War II. In 1969, Fort McClary was added to the National Register of Historic Places. In 1987, the blockhouse and other structures underwent renovation, with the blockhouse now serving as a museum.

NOTES:

PASSPORT STAMPS

FORT O'BRIEN STATE HISTORIC SITE

COUNTY: WASHINGTON		ESTABLISHED: 1923		AREA (AC/HA): 2 / 0.8
DATE VISITED:	LODGING:		WHO I WENT WITH:	
WEATHER: ☀☐ ☁☐ ☂☐ ❄☐ ⛅☐ ☁☐			SPRING ☐ SUMMER ☐ FALL ☐ WINTER ☐	
FEE(S):	RATING: ☆ ☆ ☆ ☆ ☆		WILL I RETURN? YES / NO	

Fort O'Brien State Historic Site, also referred to as Fort Machias, is situated on the western shoreline of the Machias River, located just north of its mouth at Machias Bay and south of the central village of Machiasport. This fort experienced a tumultuous history, being constructed and demolished three times within a span of 90 years. It played a role in military engagements during the American Revolutionary War and the War of 1812, and its significance led to its inclusion on the National Register of Historic Places. Presently, the site is under the management of the Maine Department of Conservation's Bureau of Parks and Lands. It is accessible to visitors from Memorial Day to Labor Day. Occupying a parcel of approximately 2 acres (0.81 hectares), the site features a small parking area and a grassy space near the riverbank where the original fortifications once stood. The location of the Civil War defenses is marked by earthworks and a flagpole, while the Revolutionary War-era earthworks, located to the north, are obscured by overgrown vegetation. During the onset of the American Revolutionary War in April 1775, the Machias area gained the attention of British authorities in besieged Boston due to its abundant lumber and supplies. An expedition was dispatched to the region to procure these resources, resulting in the naval Battle of Machias on June 11–12, 1775. In this engagement, the colonists, led by Jeremiah O'Brien, captured a small Royal Navy ship, leading to the fort's namesake. Subsequently, a series of fortifications were established along the Machias River, including a four-gun battery at this particular location. However, this fortification was destroyed when the British forces returned in 1777, sparking a second battle. During the War of 1812, American forces occupied the fort and utilized it as a place to detain British prisoners of war brought in by privateers. In 1814, the British once again attacked Machias, destroying the fortification and burning its barracks. In 1863, a five-gun battery was installed at the site during the American Civil War, although it did not see any active combat. Although the military equipment has been removed, a 12-pound "Napoleon" cannon from the Civil War era now stands at the site. In 1923, the fortification was transferred from the federal government to the state through a deed.

NOTES:

PASSPORT STAMPS

FORT POPHAM STATE HISTORIC SITE

COUNTY: SAGADAHOC	ESTABLISHED: 1969	AREA (AC/HA): - / -

DATE VISITED:	LODGING:	WHO I WENT WITH:

WEATHER: ☀☐ ☁☐ ☔☐ ❄☐ ⛅☐ 🌫☐   SPRING ☐ SUMMER ☐ FALL ☐ WINTER ☐

FEE(S):	RATING: ☆ ☆ ☆ ☆ ☆	WILL I RETURN? YES / NO

Fort Popham is a historic fortification that dates back to the Civil War era. Situated at the mouth of the Kennebec River in Phippsburg, it holds a prominent position within sight of the former Popham Colony, which was established for a brief period. The fort, like the colony, takes its name from George Popham, the leader of the ill-fated settlement. Today, the site is preserved and managed as Fort Popham State Historic Site. During the American Revolution, there was a small fortification present at the current site of Fort Popham. In 1808, as part of the Second System of fortifications established to safeguard the coast, the federal government constructed a battery capable of accommodating field carriages for guns at this location. These forts and batteries were built in response to Thomas Jefferson's Embargo Act of 1807, which aimed to exert pressure on Britain and France by prohibiting all exports from the United States. Some of these forts were initially used to enforce the embargo. However, the embargo was highly unpopular in New England and had detrimental economic effects on the region. It was repealed in March 1809, but tensions with Britain eventually led to the War of 1812. These forts were seen not only as defensive measures but also as tools to enforce the embargo, earning them the nickname "embargo forts." The battery at the present site of Fort Popham was referred to as the "Battery on Hunnewell's Point" or the "Georgetown Battery" (at that time, Georgetown included Phippsburg). In 1811, it was described as an enclosed work with six heavy guns, a small magazine, and wooden barracks for 40 soldiers. The battery remained manned until 1815 and saw limited action during the War of 1812. After the war, four of the guns were relocated to a new battery at Cox's Head, situated north of Fort Popham on the west bank of the Kennebec River. This new battery was a brick fort with barracks capable of accommodating 105 men. The construction of Fort Popham was authorized in 1857 as part of the Third System of fortifications, although actual construction did not commence until 1861. The fort was constructed using granite blocks sourced from nearby Fox and Dix Islands. Its prominent feature was a 30-foot-high wall facing the mouth of the Kennebec River, and it was designed in a crescent shape with a circumference of approximately 500 feet. During the final months of the American Civil War, from October 1864 to July 1865, the fort was occupied by the 7th Unassigned Company of Maine Infantry. This company was led by Captain Augustin Thompson, who is notable as the inventor of Moxie soda. Originally, Fort Popham was intended to house 42 heavy guns, a combination of 10-inch and 15-inch Rodman guns. However, construction came to a halt in 1869 with only two of the planned three tiers completed. In the late 19th century, the armament of Fort Popham consisted of 36 Rodman guns and several 300-pounder (10-inch) and smaller Parrott rifles. One of the Rodman guns was donated to the town of Bowdoinham as a memorial to its soldiers who lost their lives in the Civil War, and it remains there to this day. Additionally, a 100-pounder (6.4-inch) Parrott rifle is located near the fort grounds, as recorded in 1903. The back side of Fort Popham was fortified with a low moated curtain, featuring a central gate and 20 musket ports. The experiences of war demonstrated that masonry forts were vulnerable to modern rifled guns. Consequently, construction at Fort Popham ceased in 1869 before the fortification was fully completed. However, additional work was carried out at a later time, and the fort was garrisoned again during the Spanish-American War and World War I. In the 1890s, as part of the Endicott program aimed at improving fortifications, new facilities were added to Fort Popham to establish a controlled minefield in the river near the fort. During the outbreak of the Spanish-American War in 1898, Congress approved emergency funds, including $3,200 to deploy mines in the Kennebec River. Following the war, in 1899, an 8-inch M1888 gun was mounted near the fort on a converted Rodman carriage, joining the four existing 15-inch Rodman guns and the remaining 100-pounder Parrott rifle near the fort. However, the 8-inch gun was later removed in 1910. This installation of modern guns was an interim measure to provide defense at vulnerable locations until the completion of the forts under the Endicott program. Fort Baldwin, constructed on the headland above Fort Popham from 1905 onward, featured longer-range guns that eventually made Fort Popham obsolete. Nevertheless, during the construction of Fort Baldwin, Fort Popham remained significant due to its minefield facilities. At some point, Fort Popham was likely part of the Coast Defenses of the Kennebec command. However, references suggest that this command was combined with the Coast Defenses of Portland before 1917. In World War I, Forts Popham and Baldwin were manned by approximately 200 soldiers from the 13th and 29th Coast Artillery companies of the Coast Defenses of Portland. Although Fort Baldwin was disarmed in 1924, it is possible that the mine facilities at Fort Popham remained operational throughout World War II, during which Fort Baldwin was re-equipped with towed artillery.

NOTES:

PASSPORT STAMPS

KATAHDIN IRON WORKS

COUNTY: PISCATAQUIS   ESTABLISHED: 1969   AREA (AC/HA): 18 / 7

DATE VISITED: LODGING: WHO I WENT WITH:

WEATHER: ☀☐ ☁☐ ☁☐ ❄☐ ⚡☐ 🌬☐   SPRING ☐ SUMMER ☐ FALL ☐ WINTER ☐

FEE(S):   RATING: ☆ ☆ ☆ ☆ ☆   WILL I RETURN?   YES / NO

Katahdin Iron Works is a state historic site, situated in an unorganized township bearing the same name. It served as an operational ironworks from 1845 to 1890. Along with the remaining kilns from the ironworks, the community had access to a railroad and boasted a 100-room hotel. The site was officially recognized and added to the National Register of Historic Places in 1969. Within the state property, you can find Gulf Hagas, a canyon located on the West Branch of the Pleasant River, which has been designated as a National Natural Landmark. Roughly a mile and a half downstream, you'll come across another national landmark known as "The Hermitage," a preserved grove of large Eastern White Pine trees spanning approximately 35 acres (14 hectares) and maintained by The Nature Conservancy. In 2003, the Appalachian Mountain Club acquired a 37,000-acre (15,000-hectare) property upstream from Gulf Hagas, which they named Katahdin Iron Works. Early European surveyor Moses Greenleaf translated the Abnaki name Munnalammonungan for the west branch of the Pleasant River as "very fine paint." In around 1820, he discovered Ore Mountain, which contained orange, yellow, and red iron oxide pigments used in Abnaki paints. This area was identified as a limonite gossan in 1843. Samuel Smith constructed a road from Brownville, Maine in 1841 and later established a company town where the West Branch of the Pleasant River flows out of Silver Lake. The town included various amenities such as the American Lumber Company sawmill, a boarding house, cooperative store, town hall, school, post office, stables, and homes for 200 families. Skilled stonemasons erected a 55-foot high rock blast furnace powered by water-driven blowers. Additionally, they constructed eighteen stone beehive kilns to convert wood into charcoal for the production of approximately 2,000 tons of pig iron annually. The gossan became the primary source of mined ore in 1845. The ore underwent roasting to eliminate sulfur dioxide. Smith sold the operation to David Pingree, who established the Katahdin Iron Works. When the sales of pig iron were slow, Pingree constructed a puddling refinery to produce wrought iron. However, the Boston market for wrought iron remained weak, leading to the suspension of iron works operations from 1857 until the increased demand for iron during the American Civil War in 1863. Following Pingree's death, a group of businessmen from Bangor, Maine formed the Piscataquis Iron Works Company to take over the operation in 1876. They renovated the boarding house, which became known as the Silver Lake Hotel, catering to tourists. In 1877, they hired a Swedish mining engineer to improve the iron quality by reducing the silicon content. To connect the town with the future Bangor and Aroostook Railroad in Milo, Maine, the 19-mile (31-km) Bangor and Katahdin Iron Works Railway was constructed in 1881. The railway commenced operations in

1882, but unfortunately, a hurricane caused sparks from the kilns to ignite a fire that resulted in significant damage to the plant. However, by 1885, a reconstructed facility was able to sell high-quality iron for railroad car wheels and cruiser engines used by the United States Navy. Production eventually ceased in 1890 due to the increasing costs associated with depleting supplies of charcoal, which made it difficult to compete with Pennsylvania producers who had access to ample quantities of coke. The gossan deposit is situated above a pyrrhotite deposit, which contains iron sulfide ore. Based on the known surface area, it is estimated that this deposit could be one of the largest sulfide deposits in the world. However, due to its rural location and the poor quality of the ore, mining operations remain economically unviable. In 1887, the Bangor and Katahdin Iron Works Railroad entered into a lease agreement with the Bangor and Piscataquis Railroad. The annual conversion of 10,000 cords (36,000 m³) of wood into charcoal led to the depletion of local forests by 1888. As a result, iron with a lower sulfur content became available from Michigan, rendering the local operations less competitive. In 1890, most of the smelting equipment was shipped to Nova Scotia. Subsequently, in 1891, the Bangor and Piscataquis Railroad was renamed the Bangor and Aroostook Railroad. Train service to Katahdin Iron Works was discontinued by the Bangor and Aroostook Railroad in 1922. However, Sara Green, the postmistress of Katahdin Iron Works, operated a flanged-wheel automobile along the abandoned tracks until the rails were removed in 1933. The state has since restored the blast furnace and one of the beehive charcoal kilns. These, along with some foundations of other buildings, are the only remaining remnants of the mill and village. The records from the mill can be accessed at the Fogler Library of the University of Maine.

NOTES:

PASSPORT STAMPS

STORER GARRISON STATE HISTORIC SITE

COUNTY: YORK	ESTABLISHED: -	AREA (AC/HA): - / -

DATE VISITED:	LODGING:	WHO I WENT WITH:

WEATHER: ☼☐ ☁☐ ☔☐ ❄☐ ⚡☐ 🌊☐   SPRING ☐ SUMMER ☐ FALL ☐ WINTER ☐

FEE(S):   RATING: ☆ ☆ ☆ ☆ ☆   WILL I RETURN? YES / NO

A plaque at this location serves as a commemoration of the Storer Garrison, reminding visitors of the prolonged conflict between British colonial settlers in the region and their French adversaries, who were supported by Native American allies. During the years of conflict between the British and French, which involved local settlers and Native American tribes aligned with opposing sides, it was common practice for threatened villages to fortify the sturdiest house in the area as a garrison. These garrisons provided a place of refuge for villagers in the event of an attack by the French and their Native American allies. The Storer Garrison, located at this site, was one such fortified house, belonging to Joseph Storer. It featured a palisade made of heavy timbers, situated about ten feet from the building, and four turrets positioned at each corner, serving as lookout towers. On June 9, 1691, just one year after the completion of the garrison, Native American sachem Moxus led a failed assault on the inhabitants, who were led by Captain James Convers, Jr. This attack, however, did not deter Madockawando, another native sachem and enemy of the English settlers, who vowed to seek revenge. He declared, "My brother Moxus has missed it now, but I will go myself the next year and have the dog Convers out of his hole." On June 10, 1692, the same day that the first woman was executed for witchcraft in Salem, Massachusetts, a group of frightened and wounded cattle rushed toward the garrison, causing local settlers to seek shelter within its protective walls. Close behind them, a force of five hundred Native Americans, including Moxus, Madockawando, Egeremet, and Worumbo (Anasagunticooks), led by French commander Labocree, attacked the Storer Garrison and two sloops in the nearby harbor. The assault lasted for two days, but despite being outnumbered, with only fifteen soldiers, fifteen male civilians, and some local women defending the garrison, the attackers failed to capture it or the ships. Labocree lost his life during the fighting, while Captain James Convers, Jr., the garrison's commander, received a promotion to major from Massachusetts Governor Phipps and was placed in charge of all Massachusetts forces in the Province of Maine. In 1904, the Sons of the American Revolution commissioned artist William E. Barry of Kennebunk (1846-1932) to create a sculpted plaque for the memorial at this site. Today, the management of the site falls under Maine's Bureau of Parks and Lands.

NOTES:

PASSPORT STAMPS

WHALEBACK SHELL MIDDEN

COUNTY: LINCOLN   **ESTABLISHED:** 1969   **AREA (AC/HA):** 11 / 4.4

DATE VISITED: **LODGING:**   **WHO I WENT WITH:**

WEATHER: ☼☐ ☁☐ ☂☐ ❄☐ ⚡☐ 🌫☐   SPRING☐ SUMMER☐ FALL☐ WINTER☐

FEE(S):   **RATING:** ☆ ☆ ☆ ☆ ☆   **WILL I RETURN?** YES / NO

The Whaleback Shell Midden is a shell dump primarily composed of oyster shells situated on the eastern side of the Damariscotta River. It has been preserved as a Maine state historic site and was included as part of the Damariscotta Oyster Shell Heaps, which were listed on the National Register of Historic Places in 1969. Other shell middens can also be found in the estuary in both Damariscotta and Newcastle. These middens formed over a period of approximately 1,000 years, spanning from 200 BC to AD 1000. Originally, the midden consisted of three main layers of shells. The individual shells in the bottom two layers were generally 5 to 8 inches (10 to 20 cm) in length. These layers were separated by a layer of soil, and the middle layer contained a mixture of animal bones. The top layer contained smaller shells. Archaeological findings suggest that different tribes of prehistoric people inhabited the area successively. The top layer of the midden was deposited by members of the Abenaki tribes who fished in the area during the summer season. Initially, the Whaleback midden extended more than thirty feet deep, with a length of over 1,650 feet (500 meters) and a width ranging from 1,320 to 1,650 feet (400 to 500 meters). Its name derives from its distinctive shape. However, only a small portion of the midden remains today, as a significant portion of it was processed into chicken feed between 1886 and 1891 by the Damariscotta Shell and Fertilizer company based in Massachusetts. Additionally, parts of the midden have been eroded due to rising sea levels or looted. As a result, the Glidden midden, located across the river in Newcastle, has now become the largest shell midden in Maine and the largest on the eastern coast of the United States north of Georgia.

NOTES:

PASSPORT STAMPS

CONTACT

ALLAGASH WILDERNESS WATERWAY
c/o Bureau of Parks and Lands
Northern Region Headquarters
106 Hogan Road
Bangor, ME 04401
(207) 941-4014

ANDROSCOGGIN RIVERLANDS
c/o Range Pond State Park
PO Box 475, Poland, ME 04274
(207) 998-4104

AROOSTOOK STATE PARK
87 State Park Road
Presque Isle, ME 04769
207 768-8341

BAXTER STATE PARK
Reservation Office 207-723-5140

BIRCH POINT STATE PARK
Birch Point State Park
c/o Camden Hills State Park
280 Belfast Rd.
Camden, Maine 04843
in season: (207) 236-3109
off season: (207) 236-0849

BRADBURY MOUNTAIN STATE PARK
Bradbury Mountain State Park
528 Hallowell Road
Pownal, ME 04069
(207) 688-4712

CAMDEN HILLS STATE PARK
Camden Hills State Park
280 Belfast Road
Camden, ME 04843
Park season: (207) 236-3109; After Labor Day: (207) 236-0849

COBSCOOK BAY STATE PARK
Cobscook Bay State Park
40 South Edmunds Road
Edmunds Twp, ME 04628
(207) 726-4412

CRESCENT BEACH STATE PARK
Crescent Beach State Park
7 Tower Drive
Cape Elizabeth, ME 04107
207 799-5871

DAMARISCOTTA LAKE STATE PARK
Damariscotta Lake State Park
8 State Park Road
Jefferson, ME 04348
Park season: (207) 549-7600

FERRY BEACH STATE PARK
Ferry Beach State Park
95 Bayview Road
Saco, ME 04072
Park season: (207) 283-0067
Memorial Day to Oct. 1
Off season: (207) 624-6080

FORT POINT STATE PARK
Fort Point State Park
c/o Bureau of Parks and Lands
106 Hogan Road
Bangor, ME 04401
(207) 941-4014

GRAFTON NOTCH STATE PARK
Grafton Notch State Park
c/o 1941 Bear River Road
Newry, ME 04261
In season, May 15 to Oct. 15,
call: (207) 824-2912; Off season: (207) 624-6080

HOLBROOK ISLAND SANCTUARY STATE PARK
Holbrook Island Sanctuary
PO Box 35
Brooksville, Maine 04617
(207) 326-4012

LAKE ST. GEORGE STATE PARK
Lake St. George State Park
278 Belfast Augusta Rd.
Liberty, ME 04949
(207) 589-4255

LAMOINE STATE PARK
Lamoine State Park
23 State Park Road
Lamoine, ME 04605
Park season: (207) 667-4778 May 15 to Oct. 15
Off season: (207) 941-4014

LILY BAY STATE PARK
Lily Bay State Park
13 Myrle's Way
Greenville, ME 04441
(207) 695-2700

MACKWORTH ISLAND
Mackworth Island State Park Trail
c/o Bradbury Mt. State Park
528 Hallowell Road
Pownal, ME 04069
(207) 688-4712

MOOSE POINT STATE PARK
Moose Point State Park
310 West Main Street
Searsport, ME 04974
Park season: (207) 548-2882

MOUNT BLUE STATE PARK
c/o Northern Region Office, Maine State Parks
106 Hogan Road, Suite 7
Bangor, ME 04401
(207) 941-4014

MOUNT KINEO STATE PARK
Mt. Blue State Park
299 Center Hill Road
Weld, ME 04285
Park season: (207) 585-2347
Fall, winter & spring: (207) 585-2261
Campground & Beach at 187 Webb Beach Rd.

OWLS HEAD LIGHT STATE PARK
c/o Camden Hills State Park
280 Belfast Road
Camden, ME 04843
In Season: (207) 236-3019
After Labor Day: (207) 236-0849

PEAKS-KENNY STATE PARK
Peaks-Kenny State Park
401 State Park Road
Dover-Foxcroft, ME 04426
Park season: (207) 564-2003 from May 15 - Oct 1
Off season: (207) 941-4014

PENOBSCOT NARROWS OBSERVATORY
Fort Knox State Historic Site
711 Fort Knox Rd.
Prospect, ME 04981
(207) 469-7719

PENOBSCOT RIVER CORRIDOR
Penobscot River Corridor
P.O. Box 619
Millinocket, ME 04462
(207) 592-1153 (Apr-Nov)
(207) 941-4014 (Dec- Mar)

POPHAM BEACH STATE PARK
Popham Beach State Park
10 Perkins Farm Lane
Phippsburg, ME 04562
(207) 389-1335

QUODDY HEAD STATE PARK
Quoddy Head State Park
973 South Lubec Rd.
Lubec, ME 04652
May 15 through October 15: (207) 733-0911
Off season: (207) 941-4014

RANGE PONDS STATE PARK
Range Pond State Park
P.O. Box 475
Poland, ME 04274
(207) 998-4104

RANGELEY LAKE STATE PARK
Rangeley Lake State Park
HC 32 Box 5000
Rangeley, ME 04970
In season: (207) 864-3858

REID STATE PARK
Reid State Park
375 Seguinland Road
Georgetown, ME 04548
(207) 371-2303

ROQUE BLUFFS STATE PARK
Roque Bluffs State Park
145 Schoppee Point Road
Roque Bluffs, ME 04654
Park season: (207) 255-3475 May 15 to Oct 1
Off season: (207) 941-4014

SCARBOROUGH BEACH STATE PARK
414 Blackpoint Road
Scarborough, ME 04074
(207) 883-2416

SEBAGO LAKE STATE PARK
Sebago Lake State Park
11 Park Access Road
Casco, ME 04015
Campground in-season: (207) 693-6613
Office: (207) 693-6231

SHACKFORD HEAD STATE PARK
Shackford Head State Park
c/o Cobscook Bay State Park
40 South Edmunds Road
Edmunds Township, ME 04628
(207) 726-4412

SWAN LAKE STATE PARK
Swan Lake State Park
100 West Park Lane
Swanville, Maine 04915
Park season: (207) 525-4404

SWANS FALLS CAMPGROUND
Campground Manager
Swan's Falls Campground
P.O. Box 600
Fryeburg, ME 04037-0378
(207) 935-3395

TWO LIGHTS STATE PARK
Two Lights State Park
7 Tower Dr.
Cape Elizabeth, ME 04107
(207) 799-5871

VAUGHAN WOODS MEMORIAL STATE PARK
Vaughan Woods Memorial State Park
28 Oldfields Road
S. Berwick, ME 03908
Park season: (207) 384-5160
Off season: (207) 490-4079 c/o the Lyman Forestry Office

WARREN ISLAND STATE PARK
Warren Island State Park
P.O. Box 105
Lincolnville, ME 04849
(207) 446-7090 May 15 - Sept. 15
(207) 941-4014 Sept. 16 - May 14

WOLFE'S NECK WOODS STATE PARK
Wolfe Neck Woods State Park
426 Wolfe's Neck Road
Freeport, ME 04032
(207) 865-4465

BIBLE POINT STATE HISTORIC SITE
Bible Point State Historic Site
c/o Bureau of Parks and Lands
106 Hogan Road
Bangor, ME 04401
(207) 941-4014

COLBURN HOUSE STATE HISTORIC SITE
c/o Southern Region Parks Office
Bureau of Parks and Lands
107 State House Station
Augusta, Maine 04333-0107
(207) 624-6080

COLONIAL PEMAQUID STATE HISTORIC SITE (FT. WILLIAM HENRY)
Colonial Pemaquid State Historic Site
P.O. Box 117
New Harbor, ME 04554
Park season*: (207) 677-2423
* Memorial Day to Labor Day

EAGLE ISLAND STATE HISTORIC SITE
Eagle Island State Historic Site
P.O. Box 161
S. Harpswell, ME 04079
(207) 624-6080 (c/o Region Office)

FORT BALDWIN STATE HISTORIC SITE
Popham Beach State Park
10 Perkins Farm Lane
Phippsburg, ME 04562
(207) 389-1335
c/o Popham Beach State Park

FORT EDGECOMB STATE HISTORIC SITE
Fort Edgecomb State Historic Site
66 Fort Road
Edgecomb, ME 04556
Park season: (207) 882-7777

FORT HALIFAX STATE HISTORIC SITE
Fort Halifax State Historic Site
c/o Bureau of Parks and Lands
106 Hogan Road
Bangor, ME 04401

FORT KENT STATE HISTORIC SITE
Fort Kent State Historic Site
c/o Aroostook State Park
87 State Park Road
Presque Isle, ME 04769
(207) 768-8341

FORT KNOX STATE HISTORIC SITE
Fort Knox State Historic Site
711 Fort Knox Rd.
Prospect, ME 04981
(207) 469-6553

FORT MCCLARY STATE HISTORIC SITE
Fort McClary State Historic Site
Kittery Point, Maine
Park season: (207) 439-2845
Off season: (207) 490-4079 c/o the Lyman Forestry Office

FORT O'BRIEN STATE HISTORIC SITE
Fort O'Brien State Historic Site
c/o Cobscook Bay State Park
40 South Edmunds Rd.
Edmunds Township, ME 04628
(207) 726-4412

FORT POPHAM STATE HISTORIC SITE
Fort Popham State Historic Site
10 Perkins Farm Land
Phippsburg, ME 04562
Park season: (207) 389-13

KATAHDIN IRON WORKS
Katahdin Iron Works State Historic Site
c/o Bureau of Parks and Lands
106 Hogan Road
Bangor, ME 04401
(207) 941-4014

STORER GARRISON STATE HISTORIC SITE
Historic Site Specialist
Bureau of Parks and Lands
22 State House Station
Augusta, ME 04333-0022
207-287-4975

WHALEBACK SHELL MIDDEN
Coastal Rivers Conservation Trust
P.O. Box 333 / 3 Round Top Ln
Damariscotta, ME 04543
(207) 563-1393

PHOTOS   PARK NAME...

PHOTOS   PARK NAME...

PHOTOS   PARK NAME...

PHOTOS   PARK NAME...

PHOTOS   PARK NAME...

PHOTOS   PARK NAME...

PHOTOS   PARK NAME...

PHOTOS   PARK NAME...

PHOTOS   PARK NAME..

PHOTOS   PARK NAME..

Thank you for purchasing my book!
I hope you enjoyed it!
If so, would you consider posting an online review?

This helps me to continue providing great products and
helps potential buyers to make confident decisions.

Thank you in advance for your review.

Write to me if you think I should improve anything
in my book:

maxkukisgalgan@gmail.com

Max Kukis Galgan

SEE OTHER BOOKS

COLORADO STATE PARKS BUCKET LIST

FLORIDA STATE PARKS BUCKET LIST

GEORGIA STATE PARKS BUCKET LIST

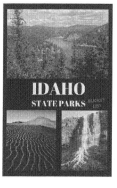

IDAHO STATE PARKS BUCKET LIST

INDIANA STATE PARKS BUCKET LIST

KANSAS STATE PARKS BUCKET LIST

MAINE STATE PARKS BUCKET LIST

MICHIGAN STATE PARKS BUCKET LIST

MINNESOTA STATE PARKS BUCKET LIST

MISSOURI
STATE PARKS BUCKET LIST

NEW YORK
STATE PARKS BUCKET LIST

OHIO
STATE PARKS BUCKET LIST

PENNSYLVANIA
STATE PARKS BUCKET LIST

TENNESSEE
STATE PARKS BUCKET LIST

TEXAS
STATE PARKS BUCKET LIST

VIRGINIA
STATE PARKS BUCKET LIST

WASHINGTON
STATE PARKS BUCKET LIST

WISCONSIN
STATE PARKS BUCKET LIST